The Poetry of Algernon Charles Swinburne

VOLUME XIII – A MIDSUMMER HOLIDAY & OTHER POEMS

Algernon Charles Swinburne was born on April 5th, 1837, in London, into a wealthy Northumbrian family. He was educated at Eton and at Balliol College, Oxford, but did not complete a degree.

In 1860 Swinburne published two verse dramas but achieved his first literary success in 1865 with Atalanta in Calydon, written in the form of classical Greek tragedy. The following year "Poems and Ballads" brought him instant notoriety. He was now identified with "indecent" themes and the precept of art for art's sake.

Although he produced much after this success in general his popularity and critical reputation declined. The most important qualities of Swinburne's work are an intense lyricism, his intricately extended and evocative imagery, metrical virtuosity, rich use of assonance and alliteration, and bold, complex rhythms.

Swinburne's physical appearance was small, frail, and plagued by several other oddities of physique and temperament. Throughout the 1860s and 1870s he drank excessively and was prone to accidents that often left him bruised, bloody, or unconscious. Until his forties he suffered intermittent physical collapses that necessitated removal to his parents' home while he recovered.

Throughout his career Swinburne also published literary criticism of great worth. His deep knowledge of world literatures contributed to a critical style rich in quotation, allusion, and comparison. He is particularly noted for discerning studies of Elizabethan dramatists and of many English and French poets and novelists. As well he was a noted essayist and wrote two novels.

In 1879, Swinburne's friend and literary agent, Theodore Watts-Dunton, intervened during a time when Swinburne was dangerously ill. Watts-Dunton isolated Swinburne at a suburban home in Putney and gradually weaned him from alcohol, former companions and many other habits as well.

Much of his poetry in this period may be inferior but some individual poems are exceptional; "By the North Sea," "Evening on the Broads," "A Nympholept," "The Lake of Gaube," and "Neap-Tide."

Swinburne lived another thirty years with Watts-Dunton. He denied Swinburne's friends access to him, controlled the poet's money, and restricted his activities. It is often quoted that 'he saved the man but killed the poet'.

Swinburne died on April 10th, 1909 at the age of seventy-two.

Index of Contents

A MIDSUMMER HOLIDAY:—
I. THE SEABOARD
II. A HAVEN
III. ON A COUNTRY ROAD

IV. THE MILL GARDEN
V. A SEA-MARK
VI. THE CLIFFSIDE PATH
VII. IN THE WATER
VIII. THE SUNBOWS
IX. ON THE VERGE
A NEW-YEAR ODE
LINES ON THE MONUMENT OF GIUSEPPE MAZZINI
LES CASQUETS
A BALLAD OF SARK
NINE YEARS OLD
AFTER A READING
MAYTIME IN MIDWINTER
A DOUBLE BALLAD OF AUGUST
HEARTSEASE COUNTRY
A BALLAD OF APPEAL
CRADLE SONGS
PELAGIUS
LOUIS BLANC
VOS DEOS LAUDAMUS
ON THE BICENTENARY OF CORNEILLE
IN SEPULCRETIS
LOVE AND SCORN
ON THE DEATH OF RICHARD DOYLE
IN MEMORY OF HENRY A. BRIGHT
A SOLITUDE
VICTOR HUGO: L'ARCHIPEL DE LA MANCHE
THE TWILIGHT OF THE LORDS
CLEAR THE WAY!
A WORD FOR THE COUNTRY
A WORD FOR THE NATION
A WORD FROM THE PSALMIST
A BALLAD AT PARTING
ALGERNON CHARLES SWINBURNE – A SHORT BIOGRAPHY
ALGERNON CHARLES SWINBURNE – A CONCISE BIBLIOGRAPHY

A MIDSUMMER HOLIDAY

TO THEODORE WATTS

THE SEABOARD

The sea is at ebb, and the sound of her utmost word
Is soft as the least wave's lapse in a still small reach.
From bay into bay, on quest of a goal deferred,
From headland ever to headland and breach to breach

Where earth gives ear to the message that all days preach
With changes of gladness and sadness that cheer and chide,
The lone way lures me along by a chance untried
That haply, if hope dissolve not and faith be whole,
Not all for nought shall I seek, with a dream for guide.
The goal that is not, and ever again the goal.

The trackless ways are untravelled of sail or bird;
The hoar wave hardly recedes from the soundless beach.
The silence of instant noon goes nigh to be heard,
The viewless void to be visible: all and each,
A closure of calm no clamour of storm can breach
Concludes and confines and absorbs them on either side,
All forces of light and of life and the live world's pride.
Sands hardly ruffled of ripples that hardly roll
Seem ever to show as in reach of a swift brief stride
The goal that is not, and ever again the goal.

The waves are a joy to the seamew, the meads to the herd,
And a joy to the heart is a goal that it may not reach.
No sense that for ever the limits of sense engird,
No hearing or sight that is vassal to form or speech,
Learns ever the secret that shadow and silence teach,
Hears ever the notes that or ever they swell subside,
Sees ever the light that lights not the loud world's tide,
Clasps ever the cause of the lifelong scheme's control
Wherethrough we pursue, till the waters of life be dried,
The goal that is not, and ever again the goal.

Friend, what have we sought or seek we, whate'er betide,
Though the seaboard shift its mark from afar descried,
But aims whence ever anew shall arise the soul?
Love, thought, song, life, but show for a glimpse and hide
The goal that is not, and ever again the goal.

A HAVEN

East and north a waste of waters, south and west
Lonelier lands than dreams in sleep would feign to be,
When the soul goes forth on travel, and is prest
Round and compassed in with clouds that flash and flee
Dells without a streamlet, downs without a tree,
Cirques of hollow cliff that crumble, give their guest
Little hope, till hard at hand he pause, to see
Where the small town smiles, a warm still sea-side nest.

Many a lone long mile, by many a headland's crest,
Down by many a garden dear to bird and bee,
Up by many a sea-down's bare and breezy breast,
Winds the sandy strait of road where flowers run free.
Here along the deep steep lanes by field and lea
Knights have carolled, pilgrims chanted, on their quest,
Haply, ere a roof rose toward the bleak strand's lee,
Where the small town smiles, a warm still sea-side nest.

Are the wild lands cursed perchance of time, or blest,
Sad with fear or glad with comfort of the sea?
Are the ruinous towers of churches fallen on rest
Watched of wanderers woful now, glad once as we,
When the night has all men's eyes and hearts in fee,
When the soul bows down dethroned and dispossest?
Yet must peace keep guard, by day's and night's decree,
Where the small town smiles, a warm still sea-side nest.

Friend, the lonely land is bright for you and me
All its wild ways through: but this methinks is best,
Here to watch how kindly time and change agree
Where the small town smiles, a warm still sea-side nest.

ON A COUNTRY ROAD

Along these low pleached lanes, on such a day,
So soft a day as this, through shade and sun,
With glad grave eyes that scanned the glad wild way,
And heart still hovering o'er a song begun,
And smile that warmed the world with benison,
Our father, lord long since of lordly rhyme,
Long since hath haply ridden, when the lime
Bloomed broad above him, flowering where he came.
Because thy passage once made warm this clime,
Our father Chaucer, here we praise thy name.

Each year that England clothes herself with May,
She takes thy likeness on her. Time hath spun
Fresh raiment all in vain and strange array
For earth and man's new spirit, fain to shun
Things past for dreams of better to be won,
Through many a century since thy funeral chime
Rang, and men deemed it death's most direful crime
To have spared not thee for very love or shame;
And yet, while mists round last year's memories climb,
Our father Chaucer, here we praise thy name.

Each turn of the old wild road whereon we stray,
Meseems, might bring us face to face with one
Whom seeing we could not but give thanks, and pray
For England's love our father and her son
To speak with us as once in days long done
With all men, sage and churl and monk and mime,
Who knew not as we know the soul sublime
That sang for song's love more than lust of fame.
Yet, though this be not, yet, in happy time,
Our father Chaucer, here we praise thy name.

Friend, even as bees about the flowering thyme,
Years crowd on years, till hoar decay begrime
Names once beloved; but, seeing the sun the same,
As birds of autumn fain to praise the prime,
Our father Chaucer, here we praise thy name.

THE MILL GARDEN

Stately stand the sunflowers, glowing down the garden-side,
Ranged in royal rank arow along the warm grey wall,
Whence their deep disks burn at rich midnoon afire with pride,
Even as though their beams indeed were sunbeams, and the tall
Sceptral stems bore stars whose reign endures, not flowers that fall.
Lowlier laughs and basks the kindlier flower of homelier fame,
Held by love the sweeter that it blooms in Shakespeare's name,
Fragrant yet as though his hand had touched and made it thrill,
Like the whole world's heart, with warm new life and gladdening flame.
Fair befall the fair green close that lies below the mill!

Softlier here the flower-soft feet of refluent seasons glide,
Lightlier breathes the long low note of change's gentler call.
Wind and storm and landslip feed the lone sea's gulf outside,
Half a seamew's first flight hence; but scarce may these appal
Peace, whose perfect seal is set for signet here on all.
Steep and deep and sterile, under fields no plough can tame,
Dip the cliffs full-fledged with poppies red as love or shame,
Wide wan daisies bleak and bold, or herbage harsh and chill;
Here the full clove pinks and wallflowers crown the love they claim.
Fair befall the fair green close that lies below the mill!

All the place breathes low, but not for fear lest ill betide,
Soft as roses answering roses, or a dove's recall.
Little heeds it how the seaward banks may stoop and slide,
How the winds and years may hold all outer things in thrall,

How their wrath may work on hoar church tower and boundary wall.
Far and wide the waste and ravin of their rule proclaim
Change alone the changeless lord of things, alone the same:
Here a flower is stronger than the winds that work their will,
Or the years that wing their way through darkness toward their aim.
Fair befall the fair green close that lies below the mill!

Friend, the home that smiled us welcome hither when we came,
When we pass again with summer, surely should reclaim
Somewhat given of heart's thanksgiving more than words fulfil—
More than song, were song more sweet than all but love, might frame.
Fair befall the fair green close that lies below the mill!

A SEA-MARK

Rains have left the sea-banks ill to climb:
Waveward sinks the loosening seaboard's floor:
Half the sliding cliffs are mire and slime.
Earth, a fruit rain-rotted to the core,
Drops dissolving down in flakes, that pour
Dense as gouts from eaves grown foul with grime.
One sole rock which years that scathe not score
Stands a sea-mark in the tides of time.

Time were even as even the rainiest clime,
Life were even as even this lapsing shore,
Might not aught outlive their trustless prime:
Vainly fear would wail or hope implore,
Vainly grief revile or love adore
Seasons clothed in sunshine, rain, or rime
Now for me one comfort held in store
Stands a sea-mark in the tides of time.

Once, by fate's default or chance's crime,
Each apart, our burdens each we bore;
Heard, in monotones like bells that chime,
Chime the sounds of sorrows, float and soar
Joy's full carols, near or far before;
Heard not yet across the alternate rhyme
Time's tongue tell what sign set fast of yore
Stands a sea-mark in the tides of time.

Friend, the sign we knew not heretofore
Towers in sight here present and sublime.
Faith in faith established evermore
Stands a sea-mark in the tides of time.

THE CLIFFSIDE PATH

Seaward goes the sun, and homeward by the down
We, before the night upon his grave be sealed.
Low behind us lies the bright steep murmuring town,
High before us heaves the steep rough silent field.
Breach by ghastlier breach, the cliffs collapsing yield:
Half the path is broken, half the banks divide;
Flawed and crumbled, riven and rent, they cleave and slide
Toward the ridged and wrinkled waste of girdling sand
Deep beneath, whose furrows tell how far and wide
Wind is lord and change is sovereign of the strand.

Star by star on the unsunned waters twiring down.
Golden spear-points glance against a silver shield.
Over banks and bents, across the headland's crown,
As by pulse of gradual plumes through twilight wheeled,
Soft as sleep, the waking wind awakes the weald.
Moor and copse and fallow, near or far descried.
Feel the mild wings move, and gladden where they glide:
Silence, uttering love that all things understand,
Bids the quiet fields forget that hard beside
Wind is lord and change is sovereign of the strand.

Yet may sight, ere all the hoar soft shade grow brown,
Hardly reckon half the lifts and rents unhealed
Where the scarred cliffs downward sundering drive and drown,
Hewn as if with stroke of swords in tempest steeled,
Wielded as the night's will and the wind's may wield.
Crowned and zoned in vain with flowers of autumn-tide,
Soon the blasts shall break them, soon the waters hide,
Soon, where late we stood, shall no man ever stand.
Life and love seek harbourage on the landward side:
Wind is lord and change is sovereign of the strand.

Friend, though man be less than these, for all his pride,
Yet, for all his weakness, shall not hope abide?
Wind and change can wreck but life and waste but land:
Truth and trust are sure, though here till all subside
Wind is lord and change is sovereign of the strand.

IN THE WATER

The sea is awake, and the sound of the song
    of the joy of her waking is rolled
From afar to the star that recedes, from anear
    to the wastes of the wild wide shore.
Her call is a trumpet compelling us homeward:
    if dawn in her east be acold,
From the sea shall we crave not her grace to rekindle
    the life that it kindled before,
Her breath to requicken, her bosom to rock us,
    her kisses to bless as of yore?
For the wind, with his wings half open, at pause
    in the sky, neither fettered nor free,
Leans waveward and flutters the ripple to laughter
    and fain would the twain of us be
Where lightly the wave yearns forward from under
    the curve of the deep dawn's dome,
And, full of the morning and fired with the pride
    of the glory thereof and the glee,
Strike out from the shore as the heart in us bids
    and beseeches, athirst for the foam.

Life holds not an hour that is better to live in:
    the past is a tale that is told,
The future a sun-flecked shadow, alive and asleep,
    with a blessing in store.
As we give us again to the waters, the rapture
    of limbs that the waters enfold
Is less than the rapture of spirit whereby,
    though the burden it quits were sore,
Our souls and the bodies they wield at their will
    are absorbed in the life they adore—
In the life that endures no burden, and bows not
    the forehead, and bends not the knee—
In the life everlasting of earth and of heaven,
    in the laws that atone and agree,
In the measureless music of things, in the fervour
    of forces that rest or that roam,
That cross and return and reissue, as I
    after you and as you after me
Strike out from the shore as the heart in us bids
    and beseeches, athirst for the foam.

For, albeit he were less than the least of them, haply
    the heart of a man may be bold
To rejoice in the word of the sea as a mother's
    that saith to the son she bore,
Child, was not the life in thee mine, and my spirit
    the breath in thy lips from of old?

Have I let not thy weakness exult in my strength,
    and thy foolishness learn of my lore?
Have I helped not or healed not thine anguish, or made not
    the might of thy gladness more?
And surely his heart should answer, The light
    of the love of my life is in thee.
She is fairer than earth, and the sun is not fairer,
    the wind is not blither than she:
From my youth hath she shown me the joy of her bays
    that I crossed, of her cliffs that I clomb,
Till now that the twain of us here, in desire
    of the dawn and in trust of the sea,
Strike out from the shore as the heart in us bids
    and beseeches, athirst for the foam.

Friend, earth is a harbour of refuge for winter,
    a covert whereunder to flee
When day is the vassal of night, and the strength
    of the hosts of her mightier than he;
But here is the presence adored of me, here
    my desire is at rest and at home.
There are cliffs to be climbed upon land, there are ways
    to be trodden and ridden, but we
Strike out from the shore as the heart in us bids
    and beseeches, athirst for the foam.

THE SUNBOWS

Spray of song that springs in April,
    light of love that laughs through May,
Live and die and live for ever:
    nought of all thing far less fair
Keeps a surer life than these
    that seem to pass like fire away.
In the souls they live which are
    but all the brighter that they were;
In the hearts that kindle, thinking
    what delight of old was there.
Wind that shapes and lifts and shifts them
    bids perpetual memory play
Over dreams and in and out
    of deeds and thoughts which seem to wear
Light that leaps and runs and revels
    through the springing flames of spray.

Dawn is wild upon the waters

where we drink of dawn to-day:
Wide, from wave to wave rekindling
    in rebound through radiant air,
Flash the fires unwoven and woven
    again of wind that works in play,
Working wonders more than heart
    may note or sight may wellnigh dare,
Wefts of rarer light than colours
    rain from heaven, though this be rare.
Arch on arch unbuilt in building,
    reared and ruined ray by ray,
Breaks and brightens, laughs and lessens,
    even till eyes may hardly bear
Light that leaps and runs and revels
    through the springing flames of spray.

Year on year sheds light and music
    rolled and flashed from bay to bay
Round the summer capes of time
    and winter headlands keen and bare
Whence the soul keeps watch, and bids
    her vassal memory watch and pray,
If perchance the dawn may quicken,
    or perchance the midnight spare.
Silence quells not music, darkness
    takes not sunlight in her snare;
Shall not joys endure that perish?
    Yea, saith dawn, though night say nay:
Life on life goes out, but very
    life enkindles everywhere
Light that leaps and runs and revels
    through the springing flames of spray.

Friend, were life no more than this is,
    well would yet the living fare.
All aflower and all afire
    and all flung heavenward, who shall say
Such a flash of life were worthless?
    This is worth a world of care—
Light that leaps and runs and revels
    through the springing flames of spray.

ON THE VERGE

Here begins the sea that ends not
    till the world's end. Where we stand,

Could we know the next high sea-mark
    set beyond these waves that gleam,
We should know what never man hath
    known, nor eye of man hath scanned.
Nought beyond these coiling clouds
    that melt like fume of shrines that steam
Breaks or stays the strength of waters
    till they pass our bounds of dream.
Where the waste Land's End leans westward,
    all the seas it watches roll
Find their border fixed beyond them,
    and a worldwide shore's control:
These whereby we stand no shore
    beyond us limits: these are free.
Gazing hence, we see the water
    that grows iron round the Pole,
From the shore that hath no shore
    beyond it set in all the sea.

Sail on sail along the sea-line
    fades and flashes; here on land
Flash and fade the wheeling wings
    on wings of mews that plunge and scream.
Hour on hour along the line
    of life and time's evasive strand
Shines and darkens, wanes and waxes,
    slays and dies: and scarce they seem
More than motes that thronged and trembled
    in the brief noon's breath and beam.
Some with crying and wailing, some
    with notes like sound of bells that toll,
Some with sighing and laughing, some
    with words that blessed and made us whole,
Passed, and left us, and we know not
    what they were, nor what were we.
Would we know, being mortal? Never
    breath of answering whisper stole
From the shore that hath no shore
    beyond it set in all the sea.

Shadows, would we question darkness?
    Ere our eyes and brows be fanned
Round with airs of twilight, washed
    with dews from sleep's eternal stream,
Would we know sleep's guarded secret?
    Ere the fire consume the brand,
Would it know if yet its ashes
    may requicken? yet we deem

Surely man may know, or ever
    night unyoke her starry team,
What the dawn shall be, or if
    the dawn shall be not, yea, the scroll
Would we read of sleep's dark scripture,
    pledge of peace or doom of dole.
Ah, but here man's heart leaps, yearning
    toward the gloom with venturous glee,
Though his pilot eye behold
    nor bay nor harbour, rock nor shoal,
From the shore that hath no shore
    beyond it set in all the sea.

Friend, who knows if death indeed
    have life or life have death for goal?
Day nor night can tell us, nor
    may seas declare nor skies unroll
What has been from everlasting,
    or if aught shall always be.
Silence answering only strikes
    response reverberate on the soul
From the shore that hath no shore
    beyond it set in all the sea.

A NEW-YEAR ODE

TO VICTOR HUGO

I

Twice twelve times have the springs of years refilled
Their fountains from the river-head of time
Since by the green sea's marge, ere autumn chilled
Waters and woods with sense of changing clime,
A great light rose upon my soul, and thrilled
My spirit of sense with sense of spheres in chime,
Sound as of song wherewith a God would build
Towers that no force of conquering war might climb.
Wind shook the glimmering sea
Even as my soul in me
Was stirred with breath of mastery more sublime,
Uplift and borne along
More thunderous tides of song,
Where wave rang back to wave more rapturous rhyme
And world on world flashed lordlier light
Than ever lit the wandering ways of ships by night.

II

The spirit of God, whose breath of life is song,
Moved, though his word was human, on the face
Of those deep waters of the soul, too long
Dumb, dark, and cold, that waited for the grace
Wherewith day kindles heaven: and as some throng
Of quiring wings fills full some lone chill place
With sudden rush of life and joy, more strong
Than death or sorrow or all night's darkling race,
So was my heart, that heard
All heaven in each deep word,
Filled full with light of thought, and waxed apace
Itself more wide and deep,
To take that gift and keep
And cherish while my days fulfilled their space;
A record wide as earth and sea,
The Legend writ of Ages past and yet to be.

III

As high the chant of Paradise and Hell
Rose, when the soul of Milton gave it wings;
As wide the sweep of Shakespeare's empire fell,
When life had bared for him her secret springs;
But not his various soul might range and dwell
Amid the mysteries of the founts of things;
Nor Milton's range of rule so far might swell
Across the kingdoms of forgotten kings.
Men, centuries, nations, time,
Life, death, love, trust, and crime,
Rang record through the change of smitten strings
That felt an exile's hand
Sound hope for every land
More loud than storm's cloud-sundering trumpet rings,
And bid strong death for judgment rise,
And life bow down for judgment of his awless eyes.

IV

And death, soul-stricken in his strength, resigned
The keeping of the sepulchres to song;
And life was humbled, and his height of mind
Brought lower than lies a grave-stone fallen along;

And like a ghost and like a God mankind
Rose clad with light and darkness; weak and strong,
Clean and unclean, with eyes afire and blind,
Wounded and whole, fast bound with cord and thong,
Free; fair and foul, sin-stained,
And sinless; crowned and chained;
Fleet-limbed, and halting all his lifetime long;
Glad of deep shame, and sad
For shame's sake; wise, and mad;
Girt round with love and hate of right and wrong;
Armed and disarmed for sleep and strife;
Proud, and sore fear made havoc of his pride of life.

V

Shadows and shapes of fable and storied sooth
Rose glorious as with gleam of gold unpriced;
Eve, clothed with heavenly nakedness and youth
That matched the morning's; Cain, self-sacrificed
On crime's first altar: legends wise as truth,
And truth in legends deep embalmed and spiced;
The stars that saw the starlike eyes of Ruth,
The grave that heard the clarion call of Christ.
And higher than sorrow and mirth
The heavenly song of earth
Sprang, in such notes as might have well sufficed
To still the storms of time
And sin's contentious clime
With peace renewed of life reparadised:
Earth, scarred not yet with temporal scars;
Goddess of gods, our mother, chosen among the stars.

VI

Earth fair as heaven, ere change and time set odds
Between them, light and darkness know not when,
And fear, grown strong through panic periods,
Crouched, a crowned worm, in faith's Lernean fen,
And love lay bound, and hope was scourged with rods,
And death cried out from desert and from den,
Seeing all the heaven above him dark with gods
And all the world about him marred of men.
Cities that nought might purge
Save the sea's whelming surge
From all the pent pollutions in their pen
Deep death drank down, and wrought,

With wreck of all things, nought,
That none might live of all their names again,
Nor aught of all whose life is breath
Serve any God whose likeness was not like to death.

VI

Till by the lips and eyes of one live nation
The blind mute world found grace to see and speak,
And light watched rise a more divine creation
At that more godlike utterance of the Greek,
Let there be freedom. Kings whose orient station
Made pale the morn, and all her presage bleak,
Girt each with strengths of all his generation,
Dim tribes of shamefaced soul and sun-swart cheek,
Twice, urged with one desire,
Son following hard on sire,
With all the wrath of all a world to wreak,
And all the rage of night
Afire against the light
Whose weakness makes her strong-winged empire weak,
Stood up to unsay that saying, and fell
Too far for song, though song were thousand-tongued, to tell.

VIII

From those deep echoes of the loud Ægean
That rolled response whereat false fear was chid
By songs of joy sublime and Sophoclean,
Fresh notes reverberate westward rose to bid
All wearier times take comfort from the pæan
That tells the night what deeds the sunrise did,
Even till the lawns and torrents Pyrenean
Ring answer from the records of the Cid.
But never force of fountains
From sunniest hearts of mountains
Wherein the soul of hidden June was hid
Poured forth so pure and strong
Springs of reiterate song,
Loud as the streams his fame was reared amid,
More sweet than flowers they feed, and fair
With grace of lordlier sunshine and more lambent air.

IX

A star more prosperous than the storm-clothed east's
Clothed all the warm south-west with light like spring's,
When hands of strong men spread the wolves their feasts
And from snake-spirited princes plucked the stings;
Ere earth, grown all one den of hurtling beasts,
Had for her sunshine and her watersprings
The fire of hell that warmed the hearts of priests,
The wells of blood that slaked the lips of kings.
The shadow of night made stone
Stood populous and alone,
Dense with its dead and loathed of living things
That draw not life from death,
And as with hell's own breath
And clangour of immitigable wings
Vexed the fair face of Paris, made
Foul in its murderous imminence of sound and shade.

X

And all these things were parcels of the vision
That moved a cloud before his eyes, or stood
A tower half shattered by the strong collision
Of spirit and spirit, of evil gods with good;
A ruinous wall rent through with grim division,
Where time had marked his every monstrous mood
Of scorn and strength and pride and self-derision:
The Tower of Things, that felt upon it brood
Night, and about it cast
The storm of all the past
Now mute and forceless as a fire subdued:
Yet through the rifted years
And centuries veiled with tears
And ages as with very death imbrued
Freedom, whence hope and faith grow strong,
Smiles, and firm love sustains the indissoluble song.

XI

Above the cloudy coil of days deceased,
Its might of flight, with mists and storms beset,
Burns heavenward, as with heart and hope increased,
For all the change of tempests, all the fret
Of frost or fire, keen fraud or force released,
Wherewith the world once wasted knows not yet
If evil or good lit all the darkling east
From the ardent moon of sovereign Mahomet.

Sublime in work and will
The song sublimer still
Salutes him, ere the splendour shrink and set;
Then with imperious eye
And wing that sounds the sky
Soars and sees risen as ghosts in concourse met
The old world's seven elder wonders, firm
As dust and fixed as shadows, weaker than the worm.

XII

High witness borne of knights high-souled and hoary
Before death's face and empire's rings and glows
Even from the dust their life poured forth left gory,
As the eagle's cry rings after from the snows
Supreme rebuke of shame clothed round with glory
And hosts whose track the false crowned eagle shows;
More loud than sounds through stormiest song and story
The laugh of slayers whose names the sea-wind knows;
More loud than peals on land
In many a red wet hand
The clash of gold and cymbals as they close;
Loud as the blast that meets
The might of marshalled fleets
And sheds it into shipwreck, like a rose
Blown from a child's light grasp in sign
That earth's high lords are lords not over breeze and brine.

XIII

Above the dust and mire of man's dejection
The wide-winged spirit of song resurgent sees
His wingless and long-labouring resurrection
Up the arduous heaven, by sore and strange degrees
Mount, and with splendour of the soul's reflection
Strike heaven's dark sovereign down upon his knees,
Pale in the light of orient insurrection,
And dumb before the almightier lord's decrees
Who bade him be of yore,
Who bids him be no more:
And all earth's heart is quickened as the sea's,
Even as when sunrise burns
The very sea's heart yearns
That heard not on the midnight-walking breeze
The wail that woke with evensong
From hearts of poor folk watching all the darkness long.

Dawn and the beams of sunbright song illume
Love, with strange children at her piteous breast,
By grace of weakness from the grave-mouthed gloom
Plucked, and by mercy lulled to living rest,
Soft as the nursling's nigh the grandsire's tomb
That fell on sleep, a bird of rifled nest;
Soft as the lips whose smile unsaid the doom
That gave their sire to violent death's arrest.
Even for such love's sake strong,
Wrath fires the inveterate song
That bids hell gape for one whose bland mouth blest
All slayers and liars that sighed
Prayer as they slew and lied
Till blood had clothed his priesthood as a vest,
And hears, though darkness yet be dumb,
The silence of the trumpet of the wrath to come.

Nor lacked these lights of constellated age
A star among them fed with life more dire,
Lit with his bloodied fame, whose withering rage
Made earth for heaven's sake one funereal pyre
And life in faith's name one appointed stage
For death to purge the souls of men with fire.
Heaven, earth, and hell on one thrice tragic page
Mixed all their light and darkness: one man's lyre
Gave all their echoes voice;
Bade rose-cheeked love rejoice,
And cold-lipped craft with ravenous fear conspire,
And fire-eyed faith smite hope
Dead, seeing enthroned as Pope
And crowned of heaven on earth at hell's desire
Sin, called by death's incestuous name
Borgia: the world that heard it flushed and quailed with shame.

Another year, and hope triumphant heard
The consummating sound of song that spake
Conclusion to the multitudinous word
Whose expectation held her spirit awake

Till full delight for twice twelve years deferred
Bade all souls entering eat and drink, and take
A third time comfort given them, that the third
Might heap the measure up of twain, and make
The sinking year sublime
Among all sons of time
And fan in all men's memories for his sake.
Each thought of ours became
Fire, kindling from his flame,
And music widening in his wide song's wake.
Yea, and the world bore witness here
How great a light was risen upon this darkening year.

XVII

It was the dawn of winter: sword in sheath,
Change, veiled and mild, came down the gradual air
With cold slow smiles that hid the doom beneath.
Five days to die in yet were autumn's, ere
The last leaf withered from his flowerless wreath.
South, east, and north, our skies were all blown bare,
But westward over glimmering holt and heath
Cloud, wind, and light had made a heaven more fair
Than ever dream or truth
Showed earth in time's keen youth
When men with angels communed unaware.
Above the sun's head, now
Veiled even to the ardent brow,
Rose two sheer wings of sundering cloud, that were
As a bird's poised for vehement flight,
Full-fledged with plumes of tawny fire and hoar grey light.

XVIII

As midnight black, as twilight brown, they spread,
But feathered thick with flame that streaked and lined
Their living darkness, ominous else of dread,
From south to northmost verge of heaven inclined
Most like some giant angel's, whose bent head
Bowed earthward, as with message for mankind
Of doom or benediction to be shed
From passage of his presence. Far behind,
Even while they seemed to close,
Stoop, and take flight, arose
Above them, higher than heavenliest thought may find
In light or night supreme

Of vision or of dream,
Immeasurable of men's eyes or mounting mind,
Heaven, manifest in manifold
Light of pure pallid amber, cheered with fire of gold.

And where the fine gold faded all the sky
Shone green as the outer sea when April glows,
Inlaid with flakes and feathers fledged to fly
Of cloud suspense in rapture and repose,
With large live petals, broad as love bids lie
Full open when the sun salutes the rose,
And small rent sprays wherewith the heavens most high
Were strewn as autumn strews the garden-close
With ruinous roseleaves whirled
About their wan chill world,
Through wind-worn bowers that now no music knows,
Spoil of the dim dusk year
Whose utter night is near,
And near the flower of dawn beyond it blows;
Till east and west were fire and light,
As though the dawn to come had flushed the coming night.

The highways paced of men that toil or play,
The byways known of none but lonely feet,
Were paven of purple woven of night and day
With hands that met as hands of friends might meet—
As though night's were not lifted up to slay
And day's had waxed not weaker. Peace more sweet
Than music, light more soft than shadow, lay
On downs and moorlands wan with day's defeat,
That watched afar above
Life's very rose of love
Let all its lustrous leaves fall, fade, and fleet,
And fill all heaven and earth
Full as with fires of birth
Whence time should feed his years with light and heat:
Nay, not life's, but a flower more strong
Than life or time or death, love's very rose of song.

Song visible, whence all men's eyes were lit
With love and loving wonder: song that glowed
Through cloud and change on souls that knew not it
And hearts that wist not whence their comfort flowed,
Whence fear was lightened of her fever-fit,
Whence anguish of her life-compelling load.
Yea, no man's head whereon the fire alit,
Of all that passed along that sunset road
Westward, no brow so drear,
No eye so dull of cheer,
No face so mean whereon that light abode,
But as with alien pride
Strange godhead glorified
Each feature flushed from heaven with fire that showed
The likeness of its own life wrought
By strong transfiguration as of living thought.

XXII

Nor only clouds of the everlasting sky,
Nor only men that paced that sunward way
To the utter bourne of evening, passed not by
Unblest or unillumined: none might say,
Of all things visible in the wide world's eye,
That all too low for all that grace it lay:
The lowliest lakelets of the moorland nigh,
The narrowest pools where shallowest wavelets play,
Were filled from heaven above
With light like fire of love,
With flames and colours like a dawn in May,
As hearts that lowlier live
With light of thoughts that give
Light from the depth of souls more deep than they
Through song's or story's kindling scroll,
The splendour of the shadow that reveals the soul.

XXIII

For, when such light is in the world, we share,
All of us, all the rays thereof that shine:
Its presence is alive in the unseen air,
Its fire within our veins as quickening wine;
A spirit is shed on all men everywhere,
Known or not known of all men for divine.
Yea, as the sun makes heaven, that light makes fair
All souls of ours, all lesser souls than thine,

Priest, prophet, seer and sage,
Lord of a subject age
That bears thy seal upon it for a sign;
Whose name shall be thy name,
Whose light thy light of fame,
The light of love that makes thy soul a shrine;
Whose record through all years to be
Shall bear this witness written—that its womb bare thee.

O mystery, whence to one man's hand was given
Power upon all things of the spirit, and might
Whereby the veil of all the years was riven
And naked stood the secret soul of night!
O marvel, hailed of eyes whence cloud is driven,
That shows at last wrong reconciled with right
By death divine of evil and sin forgiven!
O light of song, whose fire is perfect light!
No speech, no voice, no thought,
No love, avails us aught
For service of thanksgiving in his sight
Who hath given us all for ever
Such gifts that man gave never
So many and great since first Time's wings took flight.
Man may not praise a spirit above
Man's: life and death shall praise him: we can only love.

Life, everlasting while the worlds endure,
Death, self-abased before a power more high,
Shall bear one witness, and their word stand sure,
That not till time be dead shall this man die
Love, like a bird, comes loyal to his lure;
Fame flies before him, wingless else to fly.
A child's heart toward his kind is not more pure,
An eagle's toward the sun no lordlier eye.
Awe sweet as love and proud
As fame, though hushed and bowed,
Yearns toward him silent as his face goes by:
All crowns before his crown
Triumphantly bow down,
For pride that one more great than all draws nigh:
All souls applaud, all hearts acclaim,
One heart benign, one soul supreme, one conquering name.

Italia, mother of the souls of men,
    Mother divine,
Of all that served thee best with sword or pen,
    All sons of thine,

Thou knowest that here the likeness of the best
    Before thee stands,
The head most high, the heart found faithfullest,
    The purest hands.

Above the fume and foam of time that flits,
    The soul, we know,
Now sits on high where Alighieri sits
    With Angelo.

Not his own heavenly tongue hath heavenly speech
    Enough to say
What this man was, whose praise no thought may reach,
    No words can weigh.

Since man's first mother brought to mortal birth
    Her first-born son,
Such grace befell not ever man on earth
    As crowns this one.

Of God nor man was ever this thing said,
    That he could give
Life back to her who gave him, whence his dead
    Mother might live.

But this man found his mother dead and slain,
    With fast sealed eyes,
And bade the dead rise up and live again,
    And she did rise.

And all the world was bright with her through him:
    But dark with strife,
Like heaven's own sun that storming clouds bedim,
    Was all his life.

Life and the clouds are vanished: hate and fear
    Have had their span
Of time to hunt, and are not: he is here,

The sunlike man.

City superb that hadst Columbus first
    For sovereign son,
Be prouder that thy breast hath later nurst
    This mightier one.

Glory be his for ever, while his land
    Lives and is free,
As with controlling breath and sovereign hand
    He bade her be.

Earth shows to heaven the names by thousands told
    That crown her fame,
But highest of all that heaven and earth behold
    Mazzini's name.

LES CASQUETS

From the depths of the waters that lighten and darken
With change everlasting of life and of death,
Where hardly by noon if the lulled ear hearken
It hears the sea's as a tired child's breath,
Where hardly by night if an eye dare scan it
The storm lets shipwreck be seen or heard,
As the reefs to the waves and the foam to the granite
Respond one merciless word,

Sheer seen and far, in the sea's live heaven,
A seamew's flight from the wild sweet land,
White-plumed with foam if the wind wake, seven
Black helms as of warriors that stir not stand.
From the depths that abide and the waves that environ
Seven rocks rear heads that the midnight masks,
And the strokes of the swords of the storm are as iron
On the steel of the wave-worn casques.

Be night's dark word as the word of a wizard,
Be the word of dawn as a god's glad word,
Like heads of the spirits of darkness visored
That see not for ever, nor ever have heard,
These basnets, plumed as for fight or plumeless,
Crowned of the storm and by storm discrowned,
Keep ward of the lists where the dead lie tombless
And the tale of them is not found.

Nor eye may number nor hand may reckon
The tithes that are taken of life by the dark,
Or the ways of the path, if doom's hand beckon,
For the soul to fare as a helmless bark—
Fare forth on a way that no sign showeth,
Nor aught of its goal or of aught between,
A path for her flight which no fowl knoweth,
Which the vulture's eye hath not seen.

Here still, though the wave and the wind seem lovers
Lulled half asleep by their own soft words,
A dream as of death in the sun's light hovers,
And a sign in the motions and cries of the birds.
Dark auguries and keen from the sweet sea-swallows
Strike noon with a sense as of midnight's breath,
And the wing that flees and the wing that follows
Are as types of the wings of death.

For here, when the night roars round, and under
The white sea lightens and leaps like fire,
Acclaimed of storm and applauded in thunder,
Sits death on the throne of his crowned desire.
Yea, hardly the hand of the god might fashion
A seat more strong for his strength to take,
For the might of his heart and the pride of his passion
To rejoice in the wars they make.

When the heart in him brightens with blitheness of battle
And the depth of its thirst is fulfilled with strife,
And his ear with the ravage of bolts that rattle,
And the soul of death with the pride of life,
Till the darkness is loud with his dark thanksgiving
And wind and cloud are as chords of his hymn,
There is nought save death in the deep night living
And the whole night worships him.

Heaven's height bows down to him, signed with his token,
And the sea's depth, moved as a heart that yearns,
Heaves up to him, strong as a heart half broken,
A heart that breaks in a prayer that burns
Of cloud is the shrine of his worship moulded,
But the altar therein is of sea-shaped stone,
Whereon, with the strength of his wide wings folded,
Sits death in the dark, alone.

He hears the word of his servant spoken,
The word that the wind his servant saith,
Storm writes on the front of the night his token,

That the skies may seem to bow down to death
But the clouds that stoop and the storms that minister
Serve but as thralls that fulfil their tasks;
And his seal is not set save here on the sinister
Crests reared of the crownless casques.

Nor flame nor plume of the storm that crowned them
Gilds or quickens their stark black strength.
Life lightens and murmurs and laughs right round them,
At peace with the noon's whole breadth and length,
At one with the heart of the soft-souled heaven,
At one with the life of the kind wild land:
But its touch may unbrace not the strengths of the seven
Casques hewn of the storm-wind's hand.

No touch may loosen the black braced helmlets
For the wild elves' heads of the wild waves wrought.
As flowers on the sea are her small green realmlets,
Like heavens made out of a child's heart's thought;
But these as thorns of her desolate places,
Strong fangs that fasten and hold lives fast:
And the vizors are framed as for formless faces
That a dark dream sees go past.

Of fear and of fate are the frontlets fashioned,
And the heads behind them are dire and dumb.
When the heart of the darkness is scarce impassioned,
Thrilled scarce with sense of the wrath to come,
They bear the sign from of old engraven,
Though peace be round them and strife seem far,
That here is none but the night-wind's haven,
With death for the harbour bar.

Of the iron of doom are the casquets carven,
That never the rivets thereof should burst.
When the heart of the darkness is hunger-starven,
And the throats of the gulfs are agape for thirst,
And stars are as flowers that the wind bids wither,
And dawn is as hope struck dead by fear,
The rage of the ravenous night sets hither,
And the crown of her work is here.

All shores about and afar lie lonely,
But lonelier are these than the heart of grief,
These loose-linked rivets of rock, whence only
Strange life scarce gleams from the sheer main reef,
With a blind wan face in the wild wan morning,
With a live lit flame on its brows by night,

That the lost may lose not its word's mute warning
And the blind by its grace have sight.

Here, walled in with the wide waste water,
Grew the grace of a girl's lone life,
The sea's and the sea-wind's foster-daughter,
And peace was hers in the main mid strife.
For her were the rocks clothed round with thunder,
And the crests of them carved by the storm-smith's craft:
For her was the mid storm rent in sunder
As with passion that wailed and laughed.

For her the sunrise kindled and scattered
The red rose-leaflets of countless cloud:
For her the blasts of the springtide shattered
The strengths reluctant of waves back-bowed.
For her would winds in the mid sky levy
Bright wars that hardly the night bade cease
At noon, when sleep on the sea lies heavy,
For her would the sun make peace.

Peace rose crowned with the dawn on golden
Lit leagues of triumph that flamed and smiled:
Peace lay lulled in the moon-beholden
Warm darkness making the world's heart mild
For all the wide waves' troubles and treasons,
One word only her soul's ear heard
Speak from stormless and storm-rent seasons,
And nought save peace was the word.

All her life waxed large with the light of it,
All her heart fed full on the sound:
Spirit and sense were exalted in sight of it,
Compassed and girdled and clothed with it round.
Sense was none but a strong still rapture,
Spirit was none but a joy sublime,
Of strength to curb and of craft to capture
The craft and the strength of Time.

Time lay bound as in painless prison
There, closed in with a strait small space.
Never thereon as a strange light risen
Change had unveiled for her grief's far face
Three white walls flung out from the basement
Girt the width of the world whereon
Gazing at night from her flame-lit casement
She saw where the dark sea shone.

Hardly the breadth of a few brief paces,
Hardly the length of a strong man's stride,
The small court flower lit with children's faces
Scarce held scope for a bud to hide.
Yet here was a man's brood reared and hidden
Between the rocks and the towers and the foam,
Where peril and pity and peace were bidden
As guests to the same sure home.

Here would pity keep watch for peril,
And surety comfort his heart with peace.
No flower save one, where the reefs lie sterile,
Gave of the seed of its heart's increase.
Pity and surety and peace most lowly
Were the root and the stem and the bloom of the flower:
And the light and the breath of the buds kept holy
That maid's else blossomless bower.

With never a leaf but the seaweed's tangle,
Never a bird's but the seamew's note,
It heard all round it the strong storms wrangle,
Watched far past it the waste wrecks float.
But her soul was stilled by the sky's endurance,
And her heart made glad with the sea's content;
And her faith waxed more in the sun's assurance
For the winds that came and went.

Sweetness was brought for her forth of the bitter
Sea's strength, and light of the deep sea's dark,
From where green lawns on Alderney glitter
To the bastioned crags of the steeps of Sark.
These she knew from afar beholden,
And marvelled haply what life would be
On moors that sunset and dawn leave golden,
In dells that smile on the sea.

And forth she fared as a stout-souled rover,
For a brief blithe raid on the bounding brine:
And light winds ferried her light bark over
To the lone soft island of fair-limbed kine.
But the league-long length of its wild green border,
And the small bright streets of serene St. Anne,
Perplexed her sense with a strange disorder
At sight of the works of man.

The world was here, and the world's confusion,
And the dust of the wheels of revolving life,
Pain, labour, change, and the fierce illusion

Of strife more vain than the sea's old strife.
And her heart within her was vexed, and dizzy
The sense of her soul as a wheel that whirled:
She might not endure for a space that busy
Loud coil of the troublous world.

Too full, she said, was the world of trouble,
Too dense with noise of contentious things,
And shews less bright than the blithe foam's bubble
As home she fared on the smooth wind's wings.
For joy grows loftier in air more lonely,
Where only the sea's brood fain would be;
Where only the heart may receive in it only
The love of the heart of the sea.

A BALLAD OF SARK

High beyond the granite portal arched across
Like the gateway of some godlike giant's hold
Sweep and swell the billowy breasts of moor and moss
East and westward, and the dell their slopes enfold
Basks in purple, glows in green, exults in gold
Glens that know the dove and fells that hear the lark
Fill with joy the rapturous island, as an ark
Full of spicery wrought from herb and flower and tree.
None would dream that grief even here may disembark
On the wrathful woful marge of earth and sea.

Rocks emblazoned like the mid shield's royal boss
Take the sun with all their blossom broad and bold.
None would dream that all this moorland's glow and gloss
Could be dark as tombs that strike the spirit acold
Even in eyes that opened here, and here behold
Now no sun relume from hope's belated spark
Any comfort, nor may ears of mourners hark
Though the ripe woods ring with golden-throated glee,
While the soul lies shattered, like a stranded bark
On the wrathful woful marge of earth and sea.

Death and doom are they whose crested triumphs toss
On the proud plumed waves whence mourning notes are tolled.
Wail of perfect woe and moan for utter loss
Raise the bride-song through the graveyard on the wold
Where the bride-bed keeps the bridegroom fast in mould,
Where the bride, with death for priest and doom for clerk,
Hears for choir the throats of waves like wolves that bark,

Sore anhungered, off the drear Eperquerie,
Fain to spoil the strongholds of the strength of Sark
On the wrathful woful marge of earth and sea.

Prince of storm and tempest, lord whose ways are dark,
Wind whose wings are spread for flight that none may mark,
Lightly dies the joy that lives by grace of thee.
Love through thee lies bleeding, hope lies cold and stark,
On the wrathful woful marge of earth and sea.

NINE YEARS OLD

FEBRUARY 4, 1883

I

Lord of light, whose shine no hands destroy,
God of song, whose hymn no tongue refuses,
Now, though spring far hence be cold and coy,
Bid the golden mouths of all the Muses
Ring forth gold of strains without alloy,
Till the ninefold rapture that suffuses
Heaven with song bid earth exult for joy,
Since the child whose head this dawn bedews is
Sweet as once thy violet-cradled boy.

II

Even as he lay lapped about with flowers,
Lies the life now nine years old before us
Lapped about with love in all its hours;
Hailed of many loves that chant in chorus
Loud or low from lush or leafless bowers,
Some from hearts exultant born sonorous,
Some scarce louder-voiced than soft-tongued showers
Two months hence, when spring's light wings poised o'er us
High shall hover, and her heart be ours.

III

Even as he, though man-forsaken, smiled
On the soft kind snakes divinely bidden
There to feed him in the green mid wild
Full with hurtless honey, till the hidden

Birth should prosper, finding fate more mild,
So full-fed with pleasures unforbidden,
So by love's lines blamelessly beguiled,
Laughs the nursling of our hearts unchidden
Yet by change that mars not yet the child.

IV

Ah, not yet! Thou, lord of night and day,
Time, sweet father of such blameless pleasure,
Time, false friend who tak'st thy gifts away,
Spare us yet some scantlings of the treasure,
Leave us yet some rapture of delay,
Yet some bliss of blind and fearless leisure
Unprophetic of delight's decay,
Yet some nights and days wherein to measure
All the joys that bless us while they may.

V

Not the waste Arcadian woodland, wet
Still with dawn and vocal with Alpheus,
Reared a nursling worthier love's regret,
Lord, than this, whose eyes beholden free us
Straight from bonds the soul would fain forget,
Fain cast off, that night and day might see us
Clear once more of life's vain fume and fret:
Leave us, then, whate'er thy doom decree us,
Yet some days wherein to love him yet.

VI

Yet some days wherein the child is ours,
Ours, not thine, O lord whose hand is o'er us
Always, as the sky with suns and showers
Dense and radiant, soundless or sonorous;
Yet some days for love's sake, ere the bowers
Fade wherein his fair first years kept chorus
Night and day with Graces robed like hours,
Ere this worshipped childhood wane before us,
Change, and bring forth fruit—but no more flowers.

VII

Love we may the thing that is to be,
Love we must; but how forego this olden
Joy, this flower of childish love, that we
Held more dear than aught of Time is holden—
Time, whose laugh is like as Death's to see—
Time, who heeds not aught of all beholden,
Heard, or touched in passing—flower or tree,
Tares or grain of leaden days or golden—
More than wind has heed of ships at sea?

VIII

First the babe, a very rose of joy,
Sweet as hope's first note of jubilation,
Passes: then must growth and change destroy
Next the child, and mar the consecration
Hallowing yet, ere thought or sense annoy,
Childhood's yet half heavenlike habitation,
Bright as truth and frailer than a toy;
Whence its guest with eager gratulation
Springs, and life grows larger round the boy.

IX

Yet, ere sunrise wholly cease to shine,
Ere change come to chide our hearts, and scatter
Memories marked for love's sake with a sign,
Let the light of dawn beholden flatter
Yet some while our eyes that feed on thine,
Child, with love that change nor time can shatter,
Love, whose silent song says more than mine
Now, though charged with elder loves and latter
Here it hails a lord whose years are nine.

AFTER A READING

For the seven times seventh time love would renew
        the delight without end or alloy
That it takes in the praise as it takes in the presence
        of eyes that fulfil it with joy;
But how shall it praise them and rest unrebuked
        by the presence and pride of the boy?

Praise meet for a child is unmeet for an elder

whose winters and springs are nine
What song may have strength in its wings to expand them,
    or light in its eyes to shine,
That shall seem not as weakness and darkness if matched
    with the theme I would fain make mine?

The round little flower of a face that exults
    in the sunshine of shadowless days
Defies the delight it enkindles to sing of it
    aught not unfit for the praise
Of the sweetest of all things that eyes may rejoice in
    and tremble with love as they gaze.

Such tricks and such meanings abound on the lips
    and the brows that are brighter than light,
The demure little chin, the sedate little nose,
    and the forehead of sun-stained white,
That love overflows into laughter and laughter
    subsides into love at the sight.

Each limb and each feature has action in tune
    with the meaning that smiles as it speaks
From the fervour of eyes and the fluttering of hands
    in a foretaste of fancies and freaks,
When the thought of them deepens the dimples that laugh
    in the corners and curves of his cheeks.

As a bird when the music within her is yet
    too intense to be spoken in song,
That pauses a little for pleasure to feel
    how the notes from withinwards throng,
So pauses the laugh at his lips for a little,
    and waxes within more strong.

As the music elate and triumphal that bids
    all things of the dawn bear part
With the tune that prevails when her passion has risen
    into rapture of passionate art,
So lightens the laughter made perfect that leaps
    from its nest in the heaven of his heart.

Deep, grave and sedate is the gaze of expectant
    intensity bent for awhile
And absorbed on its aim as the tale that enthralls him
    uncovers the weft of its wile,
Till the goal of attention is touched, and expectancy
    kisses delight in a smile.

And it seems to us here that in Paradise hardly
  the spirit of Lamb or of Blake
May hear or behold aught sweeter than lightens
  and rings when his bright thoughts break
In laughter that well might lure them to look,
  and to smile as of old for his sake.

O singers that best loved children, and best
  for their sakes are beloved of us here,
In the world of your life everlasting, where love
  has no thorn and desire has no fear,
All else may be sweeter than aught is on earth,
  nought dearer than these are dear.

MAYTIME IN MIDWINTER

A new year gleams on us, tearful
And troubled and smiling dim
As the smile on a lip still fearful,
As glances of eyes that swim:
But the bird of my heart makes cheerful
The days that are bright for him.

Child, how may a man's love merit
The grace you shed as you stand,
The gift that is yours to inherit?
Through you are the bleak days bland;
Your voice is a light to my spirit;
You bring the sun in your hand.

The year's wing shows not a feather
As yet of the plumes to be;
Yet here in the shrill grey weather
The spring's self stands at my knee,
And laughs as we commune together,
And lightens the world we see.

The rains are as dews for the christening
Of dawns that the nights benumb:
The spring's voice answers me listening
For speech of a child to come,
While promise of music is glistening
On lips that delight keeps dumb.

The mists and the storms receding
At sight of you smile and die:

Your eyes held wide on me reading
Shed summer across the sky:
Your heart shines clear for me, heeding
No more of the world than I.

The world, what is it to you, dear,
And me, if its face be grey,
And the new-born year be a shrewd year
For flowers that the fierce winds fray?
You smile, and the sky seems blue, dear;
You laugh, and the month turns May.

Love cares not for care, he has daffed her
Aside as a mate for guile:
The sight that my soul yearns after
Feeds full my sense for awhile;
Your sweet little sun-faced laughter,
Your good little glad grave smile.

Your hands through the bookshelves flutter;
Scott, Shakespeare, Dickens, are caught;
Blake's visions, that lighten and mutter;
Molière—and his smile has nought
Left on it of sorrow, to utter
The secret things of his thought.

No grim thing written or graven
But grows, if you gaze on it, bright;
A lark's note rings from the raven,
And tragedy's robe turns white;
And shipwrecks drift into haven;
And darkness laughs, and is light.

Grief seems but a vision of madness;
Life's key-note peals from above
With nought in it more of sadness
Than broods on the heart of a dove:
At sight of you, thought grows gladness,
And life, through love of you, love.

A DOUBLE BALLAD OF AUGUST

(1884)

All Afric, winged with death and fire,
Pants in our pleasant English air.

Each blade of grass is tense as wire,
And all the wood's loose trembling hair
Stark in the broad and breathless glare
Of hours whose touch wastes herb and tree.
This bright sharp death shines everywhere;
Life yearns for solace toward the sea.

Earth seems a corpse upon the pyre;
The sun, a scourge for slaves to bear.
All power to fear, all keen desire,
Lies dead as dreams of days that were
Before the new-born world lay bare
In heaven's wide eye, whereunder we
Lie breathless till the season spare:
Life yearns for solace toward the sea.

Fierce hours, with ravening fangs that tire
On spirit and sense, divide and share
The throbs of thoughts that scarce respire,
The throes of dreams that scarce forbear
One mute immitigable prayer
For cold perpetual sleep to be
Shed snowlike on the sense of care.
Life yearns for solace toward the sea.

The dust of ways where men suspire
Seems even the dust of death's dim lair.
But though the feverish days be dire
The sea-wind rears and cheers its fair
Blithe broods of babes that here and there
Make the sands laugh and glow for glee
With gladder flowers than gardens wear.
Life yearns for solace toward the sea.

The music dies not off the lyre
That lets no soul alive despair.
Sleep strikes not dumb the breathless choir
Of waves whose note bids sorrow spare.
As glad they sound, as fast they fare,
As when fate's word first set them free
And gave them light and night to wear.
Life yearns for solace toward the sea.

For there, though night and day conspire
To compass round with toil and snare
And changeless whirl of change, whose gyre
Draws all things deathwards unaware,
The spirit of life they scourge and scare,

Wild waves that follow on waves that flee
Laugh, knowing that yet, though earth despair,
Life yearns for solace toward the sea.

HEARTSEASE COUNTRY

TO ISABEL SWINBURNE

The far green westward heavens are bland,
The far green Wiltshire downs are clear
As these deep meadows hard at hand:
The sight knows hardly far from near,
Nor morning joy from evening cheer.
In cottage garden-plots their bees
Find many a fervent flower to seize
And strain and drain the heart away
From ripe sweet-williams and sweet-peas
At every turn on every way.

But gladliest seems one flower to expand
Its whole sweet heart all round us here;
'Tis Heartsease Country, Pansy Land.
Nor sounds nor savours harsh and drear
Where engines yell and halt and veer
Can vex the sense of him who sees
One flower-plot midway, that for trees
Has poles, and sheds all grimed or grey
For bowers like those that take the breeze
At every turn on every way.

Content even there they smile and stand,
Sweet thought's heart-easing flowers, nor fear,
With reek and roaring steam though fanned,
Nor shrink nor perish as they peer.
The heart's eye holds not those more dear
That glow between the lanes and leas
Where'er the homeliest hand may please
To bid them blossom as they may
Where light approves and wind agrees
At every turn on every way.

Sister, the word of winds and seas
Endures not as the word of these
Your wayside flowers whose breath would say
How hearts that love may find heart's ease
At every turn on every way.

A BALLAD OF APPEAL

TO CHRISTINA G. ROSSETTI

Song wakes with every wakening year
From hearts of birds that only feel
Brief spring's deciduous flower-time near:
And song more strong to help or heal
Shall silence worse than winter seal?
From love-lit thought's remurmuring cave
The notes that rippled, wave on wave,
Were clear as love, as faith were strong;
And all souls blessed the soul that gave
Sweet water from the well of song.

All hearts bore fruit of joy to hear,
All eyes felt mist upon them steal
For joy's sake, trembling toward a tear,
When, loud as marriage-bells that peal,
Or flutelike soft, or keen like steel,
Sprang the sheer music; sharp or grave,
We heard the drift of winds that drave,
And saw, swept round by ghosts in throng,
Dark rocks, that yielded, where they clave,
Sweet water from the well of song.

Blithe verse made all the dim sense clear
That smiles of babbling babes conceal:
Prayer's perfect heart spake here: and here
Rose notes of blameless woe and weal,
More soft than this poor song's appeal.
Where orchards bask, where cornfields wave,
They dropped like rains that cleanse and lave,
And scattered all the year along,
Like dewfall on an April grave,
Sweet water from the well of song.

Ballad, go bear our prayer, and crave
Pardon, because thy lowlier stave
Can do this plea no right, but wrong.
Ask nought beside thy pardon, save
Sweet water from the well of song.

CRADLE SONGS

(TO A TUNE OF BLAKE'S)

I

Baby, baby bright,
Sleep can steal from sight
Little of your light:

Soft as fire in dew,
Still the life in you
Lights your slumber through.

Four white eyelids keep
Fast the seal of sleep
Deep as love is deep:

Yet, though closed it lies,
Love behind them spies
Heaven in two blue eyes.

II

Baby, baby dear,
Earth and heaven are near
Now, for heaven is here.

Heaven is every place
Where your flower-sweet face
Fills our eyes with grace.

Till your own eyes deign
Earth a glance again,
Earth and heaven are twain.

Now your sleep is done,
Shine, and show the sun
Earth and heaven are one.

III

Baby, baby sweet,
Love's own lips are meet
Scarce to kiss your feet.

Hardly love's own ear,
When your laugh crows clear,
Quite deserves to hear.

Hardly love's own wile,
Though it please awhile,
Quite deserves your smile.

Baby full of grace,
Bless us yet a space:
Sleep will come apace.

IV

Baby, baby true,
Man, whate'er he do,
May deceive not you.

Smiles whose love is guile,
Worn a flattering while,
Win from you no smile.

One, the smile alone
Out of love's heart grown,
Ever wins your own.

Man, a dunce uncouth,
Errs in age and youth:
Babies know the truth.

V

Baby, baby fair,
Love is fain to dare
Bless your haughtiest air.

Baby blithe and bland,
Reach but forth a hand
None may dare withstand;

Love, though wellnigh cowed,
Yet would praise aloud
Pride so sweetly proud.

No! the fitting word
Even from breeze or bird

Never yet was heard.

VI

Baby, baby kind,
Though no word we find,
Bear us yet in mind.

Half a little hour,
Baby bright in bower,
Keep this thought aflower—

Love it is, I see,
Here with heart and knee
Bows and worships me.

What can baby do,
Then, for love so true?—
Let it worship you.

VI

Baby, baby wise,
Love's divine surmise
Lights your constant eyes.

Day and night and day
One mute word would they,
As the soul saith, say.

Trouble comes and goes;
Wonder ebbs and flows;
Love remains and glows.

As the fledgeling dove
Feels the breast above,
So your heart feels love.

PELAGIUS

I

The sea shall praise him and the shores bear part

That reared him when the bright south world was black
With fume of creeds more foul than hell's own rack,
Still darkening more love's face with loveless art
Since Paul, faith's fervent Antichrist, of heart
Heroic, haled the world vehemently back
From Christ's pure path on dire Jehovah's track,
And said to dark Elisha's Lord, 'Thou art.'
But one whose soul had put the raiment on
Of love that Jesus left with James and John
Withstood that Lord whose seals of love were lies,
Seeing what we see—how, touched by Truth's bright rod,
The fiend whom Jews and Africans called God
Feels his own hell take hold on him, and dies.

II

The world has no such flower in any land,
And no such pearl in any gulf the sea,
As any babe on any mother's knee.
But all things blessed of men by saints are banned:
God gives them grace to read and understand
The palimpsest of evil, writ where we,
Poor fools and lovers but of love, can see
Nought save a blessing signed by Love's own hand.
The smile that opens heaven on us for them
Hath sin's transmitted birthmark hid therein:
The kiss it craves calls down from heaven a rod.
If innocence be sin that Gods condemn,
Praise we the men who so being born in sin
First dared the doom and broke the bonds of God.

III

Man's heel is on the Almighty's neck who said,
Let there be hell, and there was hell—on earth.
But not for that may men forget their worth—
Nay, but much more remember them—who led
The living first from dwellings of the dead,
And rent the cerecloths that were wont to engirth
Souls wrapped and swathed and swaddled from their birth
With lies that bound them fast from heel to head.
Among the tombs when wise men all their lives
Dwelt, and cried out, and cut themselves with knives,
These men, being foolish, and of saints abhorred,
Beheld in heaven the sun by saints reviled,
Love, and on earth one everlasting Lord

In every likeness of a little child.

THREE SONNETS TO HIS MEMORY

I

The stainless soul that smiled through glorious eyes;
The bright grave brow whereon dark fortune's blast
Might blow, but might not bend it, nor o'ercast,
Save for one fierce fleet hour of shame, the skies
Thrilled with warm dreams of worthier days to rise
And end the whole world's winter; here at last,
If death be death, have passed into the past;
If death be life, live, though their semblance dies.
Hope and high faith inviolate of distrust
Shone strong as life inviolate of the grave
Through each bright word and lineament serene.
Most loving righteousness and love most just
Crowned, as day crowns the dawn-enkindled wave,
With visible aureole thine unfaltering mien.

II

Strong time and fire-swift change, with lightnings clad
And shod with thunders of reverberate years,
Have filled with light and sound of hopes and fears
The space of many a season, since I had
Grace of good hap to make my spirit glad,
Once communing with thine: and memory hears
The bright voice yet that then rejoiced mine ears,
Sees yet the light of eyes that spake, and bade
Fear not, but hope, though then time's heart were weak
And heaven by hell shade-stricken, and the range
Of high-born hope made questionable and strange
As twilight trembling till the sunlight speak.
Thou sawest the sunrise and the storm in one
Break: seest thou now the storm-compelling sun?

III

Surely thou seest, O spirit of light and fire,
Surely thou canst not choose, O soul, but see

The days whose dayspring was beheld of thee
Ere eyes less pure might have their hope's desire,
Beholding life in heaven again respire
Where men saw nought that was or was to be,
Save only death imperial. Thou and he
Who has the heart of all men's hearts for lyre,
Ye twain, being great of spirit as time is great,
And sure of sight as truth's own heavenward eye,
Beheld the forms of forces passing by
And certitude of equal-balanced fate,
Whose breath forefelt makes darkness palpitate,
And knew that light should live and darkness die.

VOS DEOS LAUDAMUS:

THE CONSERVATIVE JOURNALIST'S ANTHEM

'As a matter of fact, no man living, or who ever lived—not CÆSAR or PERICLES, not SHAKESPEARE or MICHAEL ANGELO—could confer honour more than he took on entering the House of Lords.'—Saturday Review, December 15, 1883.

'Clumsy and shallow snobbery—can do no hurt.'—Ibid.

I

O Lords our Gods, beneficent, sublime,
In the evening, and before the morning flames,
We praise, we bless, we magnify your names.
The slave is he that serves not; his the crime
And shame, who hails not as the crown of Time
That House wherein the all-envious world acclaims
Such glory that the reflex of it shames
All crowns bestowed of men for prose or rhyme.
The serf, the cur, the sycophant is he
Who feels no cringing motion twitch his knee
When from a height too high for Shakespeare nods
The wearer of a higher than Milton's crown.
Stoop, Chaucer, stoop: Keats, Shelley, Burns, bow down:
These have no part with you, O Lords our Gods.

II

O Lords our Gods, it is not that ye sit
Serene above the thunder, and exempt
From strife of tongues and casualties that tempt

Men merely found by proof of manhood fit
For service of their fellows: this is it
Which sets you past the reach of Time's attempt,
Which gives us right of justified contempt
For commonwealths built up by mere men's wit:
That gold unlocks not, nor may flatteries ope,
The portals of your heaven; that none may hope
With you to watch how life beneath you plods,
Save for high service given, high duty done;
That never was your rank ignobly won:
For this we give you praise, O Lords our Gods.

III

O Lords our Gods, the times are evil: you
Redeem the time, because of evil days.
While abject souls in servitude of praise
Bow down to heads untitled, and the crew
Whose honour dwells but in the deeds they do,
From loftier hearts your nobler servants raise
More manful salutation: yours are bays
That not the dawn's plebeian pearls bedew;
Yours, laurels plucked not of such hands as wove
Old age its chaplet in Colonos' grove.
Our time, with heaven and with itself at odds,
Makes all lands else as seas that seethe and boil;
But yours are yet the corn and wine and oil,
And yours our worship yet, O Lords our Gods.

December 15.

ON THE BICENTENARY OF CORNEILLE

CELEBRATED UNDER THE PRESIDENCY OF VICTOR HUGO

Scarce two hundred years are gone, and the world is past away
As a noise of brawling wind, as a flash of breaking foam,
That beheld the singer born who raised up the dead of Rome;
And a mightier now than he bids him too rise up to-day,
All the dim great age is dust, and its king is tombless clay,
But its loftier laurel green as in living eyes it clomb,
And his memory whom it crowned hath his people's heart for home,
And the shade across it falls of a lordlier-flowering bay.

Stately shapes about the tomb of their mighty maker pace,

Heads of high-plumed Spaniards shine, souls revive of Roman race,
Sound of arms and words of wail through the glowing darkness rise,
Speech of hearts heroic rings forth of lips that know not breath,
And the light of thoughts august fills the pride of kindling eyes
Whence of yore the spell of song drove the shadow of darkling death.

IN SEPULCRETIS

'Vidistis ipso rapere de rogo coenam.'—CATULLUS, LIX. 3.

'To publish even one line of an author which he himself has not intended for the public at large—especially letters which are addressed to private persons—is to commit a despicable act of felony.'—**HEINE**.

I

It is not then enough that men who give
The best gifts given of man to man should feel,
Alive, a snake's head ever at their heel:
Small hurt the worms may do them while they live—
Such hurt as scorn for scorn's sake may forgive.
But now, when death and fame have set one seal
On tombs whereat Love, Grief, and Glory kneel,
Men sift all secrets, in their critic sieve,
Of graves wherein the dust of death might shrink
To know what tongues defile the dead man's name
With loathsome love, and praise that stings like shame.
Rest once was theirs, who had crossed the mortal brink:
No rest, no reverence now: dull fools undress
Death's holiest shrine, life's veriest nakedness.

II

A man was born, sang, suffered, loved, and died.
Men scorned him living: let us praise him dead.
His life was brief and bitter, gently led
And proudly, but with pure and blameless pride.
He wrought no wrong toward any; satisfied
With love and labour, whence our souls are fed
With largesse yet of living wine and bread.
Come, let us praise him: here is nought to hide.
Make bare the poor dead secrets of his heart,
Strip the stark-naked soul, that all may peer,
Spy, smirk, sniff, snap, snort, snivel, snarl, and sneer:
Let none so sad, let none so sacred part

Lie still for pity, rest unstirred for shame,
But all be scanned of all men. This is fame.

III

'Now, what a thing it is to be an ass!'[1]
If one, that strutted up the brawling streets
As foreman of the flock whose concourse greets
Men's ears with bray more dissonant than brass,
Would change from blame to praise as coarse and crass
His natural note, and learn the fawning feats
Of lapdogs, who but knows what luck he meets?
But all in vain old fable holds her glass.

Mocked and reviled by men of poisonous breath,
A great man dies: but one thing worst was spared,
Not all his heart by their base hands lay bared.
One comes to crown with praise the dust of death;
And lo, through him this worst is brought to pass.
Now, what a thing it is to be an ass!

[Footnote 1: Titus Andronicus, Act iv., Scene 2.]

IV

Shame, such as never yet dealt heavier stroke
On heads more shameful, fall on theirs through whom
Dead men may keep inviolate not their tomb,
But all its depths these ravenous grave-worms choke
And yet what waste of wrath were this, to invoke
Shame on the shameless? Even their twin-born doom,
Their native air of life, a carrion fume,
Their natural breath of love, a noisome smoke,
The bread they break, the cup whereof they drink,
The record whose remembrance damns their name,
Smells, tastes, and sounds of nothing but of shame.
If thankfulness nor pity bids them think
What work is this of theirs, and pause betimes,
Not Shakespeare's grave would scare them off with rhymes.

LOVE AND SCORN

I

Love, loyallest and lordliest born of things,
Immortal that shouldst be, though all else end,
In plighted hearts of fearless friend with friend,
Whose hand may curb or clip thy plume-plucked wings?
Not grief's nor time's: though these be lords and kings
Crowned, and their yoke bid vassal passions bend,
They may not pierce the spirit of sense, or blend
Quick poison with the soul's live watersprings.
The true clear heart whose core is manful trust
Fears not that very death may turn to dust
Love lit therein as toward a brother born,
If one touch make not all its fine gold rust,
If one breath blight not all its glad ripe corn,
And all its fire be turned to fire of scorn.

II

Scorn only, scorn begot of bitter proof
By keen experience of a trustless heart,
Bears burning in her new-born hand the dart
Wherewith love dies heart-stricken, and the roof
Falls of his palace, and the storied woof
Long woven of many a year with life's whole art
Is rent like any rotten weed apart,
And hardly with reluctant eyes aloof
Cold memory guards one relic scarce exempt
Yet from the fierce corrosion of contempt,
And hardly saved by pity. Woe are we
That once we loved, and love not; but we know
The ghost of love, surviving yet in show,
Where scorn has passed, is vain as grief must be.

III

O sacred, just, inevitable scorn,
Strong child of righteous judgment, whom with grief
The rent heart bears, and wins not yet relief,
Seeing of its pain so dire a portent born,
Must thou not spare one sheaf of all the corn,
One doit of all the treasure? not one sheaf,
Not one poor doit of all? not one dead leaf
Of all that fell and left behind a thorn?
Is man so strong that one should scorn another?
Is any as God, not made of mortal mother,
That love should turn in him to gall and flame?
Nay: but the true is not the false heart's brother:

Love cannot love disloyalty: the name
That else it wears is love no more, but shame.

ON THE DEATH OF RICHARD DOYLE

A light of blameless laughter, fancy-bred,
Soft-souled and glad and kind as love or sleep,
Fades, and sweet mirth's own eyes are fain to weep
Because her blithe and gentlest bird is dead.
Weep, elves and fairies all, that never shed
Tear yet for mortal mourning: you that keep
The doors of dreams whence nought of ill may creep,
Mourn once for one whose lips your honey fed.
Let waters of the Golden River steep
The rose-roots whence his grave blooms rosy-red
And murmuring of Hyblæan hives be deep
About the summer silence of its bed,
And nought less gracious than a violet peep
Between the grass grown greener round his head.

IN MEMORY OF HENRY A. BRIGHT

Yet again another, ere his crowning year,
Gone from friends that here may look for him no more.
Never now for him shall hope set wide the door,
Hope that hailed him hither, fain to greet him here.
All the gracious garden-flowers he held so dear,
Oldworld English blossoms, all his homestead store,
Oldworld grief had strewn them round his bier of yore,
Bidding each drop leaf by leaf as tear by tear;
Rarer lutes than mine had borne more tuneful token,
Touched by subtler hands than echoing time can wrong,
Sweet as flowers had strewn his graveward path along.
Now may no such old sweet dirges more be spoken,
Now the flowers whose breath was very song are broken,
Nor may sorrow find again so sweet a song.

A SOLITUDE

Sea beyond sea, sand after sweep of sand,
Here ivory smooth, here cloven and ridged with flow
Of channelled waters soft as rain or snow,

Stretch their lone length at ease beneath the bland
Grey gleam of skies whose smile on wave and strand
Shines weary like a man's who smiles to know
That now no dream can mock his faith with show,
Nor cloud for him seem living sea or land.

Is there an end at all of all this waste,
These crumbling cliffs defeatured and defaced,
These ruinous heights of sea-sapped walls that slide
Seaward with all their banks of bleak blown flowers
Glad yet of life, ere yet their hope subside
Beneath the coil of dull dense waves and hours?

VICTOR HUGO: L'ARCHIPEL DE LA MANCHE

Sea and land are fairer now, nor aught is all the same,
Since a mightier hand than Time's hath woven their votive wreath.
Rocks as swords half drawn from out the smooth wave's jewelled sheath,
Fields whose flowers a tongue divine hath numbered name by name,
Shores whereby the midnight or the noon clothed round with flame
Hears the clamour jar and grind which utters from beneath
Cries of hungering waves like beasts fast bound that gnash their teeth,
All of these the sun that lights them lights not like his fame;
None of these is but the thing it was before he came
Where the darkling overfalls like dens of torment seethe,
High on tameless moorlands, down in meadows bland and tame,
Where the garden hides, and where the wind uproots the heath,
Glory now henceforth for ever, while the world shall be,
Shines, a star that keeps not time with change on earth and sea.

THE TWILIGHT OF THE LORDS

I

Is the sound a trumpet blown, or a bell for burial tolled,
Whence the whole air vibrates now to the clash of words like swords—
'Let us break their bonds in sunder, and cast away their cords;
Long enough the world has mocked us, and marvelled to behold
How the grown man bears the curb whence his boyhood was controlled'?
Nay, but hearken: surer counsel more sober speech affords:
'Is the past not all inscribed with the praises of our Lords?
Is the memory dead of deeds done of yore, the love grown cold
That should bind our hearts to trust in their counsels wise and bold?
These that stand against you now, senseless crowds and heartless hordes,

Are not these the sons of men that withstood your kings of old?
Theirs it is to bind and loose; theirs the key that knows the wards,
Theirs the staff to lead or smite; yours, the spades and ploughs and hods:
Theirs to hear and yours to cry, Power is yours, O Lords our Gods.'

II

Hear, O England: these are they that would counsel thee aright.
Wouldst thou fain have all thy sons sons of thine indeed, and free?
Nay, but then no more at all as thou hast been shalt thou be:
Needs must many dwell in darkness, that some may look on light;
Needs must poor men brook the wrong that ensures the rich man's right.
How shall kings and lords be worshipped, if no man bow the knee?
How, if no man worship these, may thy praise endure with thee?
How, except thou trust in these, shall thy name not lose its might?
These have had their will of thee since the Norman came to smite:
Sires on grandsires, even as wave after wave along the sea,
Sons on sires have followed, steadfast as clouds or hours in flight.
Time alone hath power to say, time alone hath eyes to see,
If your walls of rule be built but of clay-compacted sods,
If your place of old shall know you no more, O Lords our Gods.

III

Through the stalls wherein ye sit sounds a sentence while we wait,
Set your house in order: is it not builded on the sand?
Set your house in order, seeing the night is hard at hand.
As the twilight of the Gods in the northern dream of fate
Is this hour that comes against you, albeit this hour come late.
Ye whom Time and Truth bade heed, and ye would not understand,
Now an axe draws nigh the tree overshadowing all the land,
And its edge of doom is set to the root of all your state.
Light is more than darkness now, faith than fear and hope than hate,
And what morning wills, behold, all the night shall not withstand.
Rods of office, helms of rule, staffs of wise men, crowns of great,
While the people willed, ye bare; now their hopes and hearts expand,
Time with silent foot makes dust of your broken crowns and rods,
And the lordship of your godhead is gone, O Lords our Gods.

CLEAR THE WAY!

Clear the way, my lords and lackeys! you have had your day.
Here you have your answer—England's yea against your nay:
Long enough your house has held you: up, and clear the way!

Lust and falsehood, craft and traffic, precedent and gold,
Tongue of courtier, kiss of harlot, promise bought and sold,
Gave you heritage of empire over thralls of old.

Now that all these things are rotten, all their gold is rust,
Quenched the pride they lived by, dead the faith and cold the lust,
Shall their heritage not also turn again to dust?

By the grace of these they reigned, who left their sons their sway:
By the grace of these, what England says her lords unsay:
Till at last her cry go forth against them—Clear the way!

By the grace of trust in treason knaves have lived and lied:
By the force of fear and folly fools have fed their pride:
By the strength of sloth and custom reason stands defied.

Lest perchance your reckoning on some latter day be worse,
Halt and hearken, lords of land and princes of the purse,
Ere the tide be full that comes with blessing and with curse.

Where we stand; as where you sit, scarce falls a sprinkling spray;
But the wind that swells, the wave that follows, none shall stay:
Spread no more of sail for shipwreck: out, and clear the way!

A WORD FOR THE COUNTRY

Men, born of the land that for ages
Has been honoured where freedom was dear,
Till your labour wax fat on its wages
You shall never be peers of a peer.
Where might is, the right is:
Long purses make strong swords.
Let weakness learn meekness:
God save the House of Lords!

You are free to consume in stagnation:
You are equal in right to obey:
You are brothers in bonds, and the nation
Is your mother—whose sons are her prey.
Those others your brothers,
Who toil not, weave, nor till,
Refuse you and use you
As waiters on their will.

But your fathers bowed down to their masters

And obeyed them and served and adored.
Shall the sheep not give thanks to their pastors?
Shall the serf not give praise to his lord?
Time, waning and gaining,
Grown other now than then,
Needs pastors and masters
For sheep, and not for men.

If his grandsire did service in battle,
If his grandam was kissed by a king,
Must men to my lord be as cattle
Or as apes that he leads in a string?
To deem so, to dream so,
Would bid the world proclaim
The dastards for bastards,
Not heirs of England's fame.

Not in spite but in right of dishonour,
There are actors who trample your boards
Till the earth that endures you upon her
Grows weary to bear you, my lords.
Your token is broken,
It will not pass for gold:
Your glory looks hoary,
Your sun in heaven turns cold.

They are worthy to reign on their brothers,
To contemn them as clods and as carles,
Who are Graces by grace of such mothers
As brightened the bed of King Charles.
What manner of banner,
What fame is this they flaunt,
That Britain, soul-smitten,
Should shrink before their vaunt?

Bright sons of sublime prostitution,
You are made of the mire of the street
Where your grandmothers walked in pollution
Till a coronet shone at their feet.
Your Graces, whose faces
Bear high the bastard's brand,
Seem stronger no longer
Than all this honest land.

But the sons of her soldiers and seamen,
They are worthy forsooth of their hire.
If the father won praise from all free men,
Shall the sons not exult in their sire?

Let money make sunny
And power make proud their lives,
And feed them and breed them
Like drones in drowsiest hives.

But if haply the name be a burden
And the souls be no kindred of theirs,
Should wise men rejoice in such guerdon
Or brave men exult in such heirs?
Or rather the father
Frown, shamefaced, on the son,
And no men but foemen,
Deriding, cry 'Well done'?

Let the gold and the land they inherit
Pass ever from hand into hand:
In right of the forefather's merit
Let the gold be the son's, and the land.
Soft raiment, rich payment,
High place, the state affords;
Full measure of pleasure,
But now no more, my lords.

Is the future beleaguered with dangers
If the poor be far other than slaves?
Shall the sons of the land be as strangers
In the land of their forefathers' graves?
Shame were it to bear it,
And shame it were to see:
If free men you be, men,
Let proof proclaim you free.

'But democracy means dissolution:
See, laden with clamour and crime,
How the darkness of dim revolution
Comes deepening the twilight of time!
Ah, better the fetter
That holds the poor man's hand
Than peril of sterile
Blind change that wastes the land.

'Gaze forward through clouds that environ;
It shall be as it was in the past.
Not with dreams, but with blood and with iron,
Shall a nation be moulded to last.'
So teach they, so preach they,
Who dream themselves the dream
That hallows the gallows

And bids the scaffold stream.

'With a hero at head, and a nation
Well gagged and well drilled and well cowed,
And a gospel of war and damnation,
Has not empire a right to be proud?
Fools prattle and tattle
Of freedom, reason, right,
The beauty of duty,
The loveliness of light.

'But we know, we believe it, we see it,
Force only has power upon earth.'
So be it! and ever so be it
For souls that are bestial by birth!
Let Prussian with Russian
Exchange the kiss of slaves:
But sea-folk are free folk
By grace of winds and waves.

Has the past from the sepulchres beckoned?
Let answer from Englishmen be—
No man shall be lord of us reckoned
Who is baser, not better, than we.
No coward, empowered
To soil a brave man's name;
For shame's sake and fame's sake,
Enough of fame and shame.

Fame needs not the golden addition;
Shame bears it abroad as a brand.
Let the deed, and no more the tradition,
Speak out and be heard through the land.
Pride, rootless and fruitless,
No longer takes and gives:
But surer and purer
The soul of England lives.

He is master and lord of his brothers
Who is worthier and wiser than they.
Him only, him surely, shall others,
Else equal, observe and obey.
Truth, flawless and awless,
Do falsehood what it can,
Makes royal the loyal
And simple heart of man.

Who are these, then, that England should hearken,

Who rage and wax wroth and grow pale
If she turn from the sunsets that darken
And her ship for the morning set sail?
Let strangers fear dangers:
All know, that hold her dear,
Dishonour upon her
Can only fall through fear.

Men, born of the landsmen and seamen
Who served her with souls and with swords,
She bids you be brothers, and free men,
And lordless, and fearless of lords.
She cares not, she dares not
Care now for gold or steel:
Light lead her, truth speed her,
God save the Commonweal!

A WORD FOR THE NATION

I

A word across the water
Against our ears is borne,
Of threatenings and of slaughter,
Of rage and spite and scorn:
We have not, alack, an ally to befriend us,
And the season is ripe to extirpate and end us:
Let the German touch hands with the Gaul,
And the fortress of England must fall;
And the sea shall be swept of her seamen,
And the waters they ruled be their graves,
And Dutchmen and Frenchmen be free men,
And Englishmen slaves.

II

Our time once more is over,
Once more our end is near:
A bull without a drover,
The Briton reels to rear,
And the van of the nations is held by his betters,
And the seas of the world shall be loosed from his fetters,
And his glory shall pass as a breath,
And the life that is in him be death;
And the sepulchre sealed on his glory

For a sign to the nations shall be
As of Tyre and of Carthage in story,
Once lords of the sea.

III

The lips are wise and loyal,
The hearts are brave and true,
Imperial thoughts and royal
Make strong the clamorous crew,
Whence louder and prouder the noise of defiance
Rings rage from the grave of a trustless alliance,
And bids us beware and be warned,
As abhorred of all nations and scorned,
As a swordless and spiritless nation,
A wreck on the waste of the waves.
So foams the released indignation
Of masterless slaves.

IV

Brute throats that miss the collar,
Bowed backs that ask the whip,
Stretched hands that lack the dollar,
And many a lie-seared lip,
Forefeel and foreshow for us signs as funereal
As the signs that were regal of yore and imperial;
We shall pass as the princes they served,
We shall reap what our fathers deserved,
And the place that was England's be taken
By one that is worthier than she,
And the yoke of her empire be shaken
Like spray from the sea.

V

French hounds, whose necks are aching
Still from the chain they crave,
In dog-day madness breaking
The dog-leash, thus may rave:
But the seas that for ages have fostered and fenced her
Laugh, echoing the yell of their kennel against her
And their moan if destruction draw near them
And the roar of her laughter to hear them;
For she knows that if Englishmen be men

Their England has all that she craves;
All love and all honour from free men,
All hatred from slaves.

VI

All love that rests upon her
Like sunshine and sweet air,
All light of perfect honour
And praise that ends in prayer,
She wins not more surely, she wears not more proudly,
Than the token of tribute that clatters thus loudly,
The tribute of foes when they meet
That rattles and rings at her feet,
The tribute of rage and of rancour,
The tribute of slaves to the free,
To the people whose hope hath its anchor
Made fast in the sea.

VII

No fool that bows the back he
Feels fit for scourge or brand,
No scurril scribes that lackey
The lords of Lackeyland,
No penman that yearns, as he turns on his pallet,
For the place or the pence of a peer or a valet,
No whelp of as currish a pack
As the litter whose yelp it gives back,
Though he answer the cry of his brother
As echoes might answer from caves,
Shall be witness as though for a mother
Whose children were slaves.

VIII

But those found fit to love her,
Whose love has root in faith,
Who hear, though darkness cover
Time's face, what memory saith,
Who seek not the service of great men or small men
But the weal that is common for comfort of all men,
Those yet that in trust have beholden
Truth's dawn over England grow golden
And quicken the darkness that stagnates

And scatter the shadows that flee,
Shall reply for her meanest as magnates
And masters by sea.

IX

And all shall mark her station,
Her message all shall hear,
When, equal-eyed, the nation
Bids all her sons draw near,
And freedom be more than tradition or faction,
And thought be no swifter to serve her than action,
And justice alone be above her,
That love may be prouder to love her,
And time on the crest of her story
Inscribe, as remembrance engraves,
The sign that subdues with its glory
Kings, princes, and slaves.

A WORD FROM THE PSALMIST

PS. XCIV. 8

I

'Take heed, ye unwise among the people:
O ye fools, when will ye understand?'
From pulpit or choir beneath the steeple,
Though the words be fierce, the tones are bland.
But a louder than the Church's echo thunders
In the ears of men who may not choose but hear,
And the heart in him that hears it leaps and wonders,
With triumphant hope astonished, or with fear
For the names whose sound was power awaken
Neither love nor reverence now nor dread;
Their strongholds and shrines are stormed and taken,
Their kingdom and all its works are dead.

II

Take heed: for the tide of time is risen:
It is full not yet, though now so high
That spirits and hopes long pent in prison
Feel round them a sense of freedom nigh,

And a savour keen and sweet of brine and billow,
And a murmur deep and strong of deepening strength.
Though the watchman dream, with sloth or pride for pillow,
And the night be long, not endless is its length.
From the springs of dawn, from clouds that sever
From the equal heavens and the eastward sea,
The witness comes that endures for ever,
Till men be brethren and thralls be free.

III

But the wind of the wings of dawn expanding
Strikes chill on your hearts as change and death.
Ye are old, but ye have not understanding,
And proud, but your pride is a dead man's breath.
And your wise men, toward whose words and signs ye hearken,
And your strong men, in whose hands ye put your trust,
Strain eyes to behold but clouds and dreams that darken,
Stretch hands that can find but weapons red with rust.
Their watchword rings, and the night rejoices,
But the lark's note laughs at the night-bird's notes—
'Is virtue verily found in voices?
Or is wisdom won when all win votes?

IV

'Take heed, ye unwise indeed, who listen
When the wind's wings beat and shift and change;
Whose hearts are uplift, whose eyeballs glisten,
With desire of new things great and strange.
Let not dreams misguide nor any visions wrong you:
That which has been, it is now as it was then.
Is not Compromise of old a god among you?
Is not Precedent indeed a king of men?
But the windy hopes that lead mislead you,
And the sounds ye hear are void and vain.
Is a vote a coat? will franchise feed you,
Or words be a roof against the rain?

V

'Eight ages are gone since kingship entered,
With knights and peers at its harnessed back,
And the land, no more in its own strength centred,
Was cast for a prey to the princely pack.

But we pared the fangs and clipped the ravening claws of it,
And good was in time brought forth of an evil thing,
And the land's high name waxed lordlier in war because of it,
When chartered Right had bridled and curbed the king.
And what so fair has the world beholden,
And what so firm has withstood the years,
As Monarchy bound in chains all golden,
And Freedom guarded about with peers?

VI

'How think ye? know not your lords and masters
What collars are meet for brawling throats?
Is change not mother of strange disasters?
Shall plague or peril be stayed by votes?
Out of precedent and privilege and order
Have we plucked the flower of compromise, whose root
Bears blossoms that shine from border again to border,
And the mouths of many are fed with its temperate fruit.
Your masters are wiser than ye, their henchmen:
Your lords know surely whereof ye have need.
Equality? Fools, would you fain be Frenchmen?
Is equity more than a word indeed?

VII

'Your voices, forsooth, your most sweet voices,
Your worthy voices, your love, your hate,
Your choice, who know not whereof your choice is,
What stays are these for a stable state?
Inconstancy, blind and deaf with its own fierce babble,
Swells ever your throats with storm of uncertain cheers:
He leans on straws who leans on a light-souled rabble;
His trust is frail who puts not his trust in peers.'
So shrills the message whose word convinces
Of righteousness knaves, of wisdom fools;
That serfs may boast them because of princes,
And the weak rejoice that the strong man rules.

VIII

True friends, ye people, are these, the faction
Full-mouthed that flatters and snails and bays,
That fawns and foams with alternate action,
And mocks the names that it soils with praise.

As from fraud and force their power had fast beginning,
So by righteousness and peace it may not stand,
But by craft of state and nets of secret spinning,
Words that weave and unweave wiles like ropes of sand
Form, custom, and gold, and laws grown hoary,
And strong tradition that guards the gate:
To these, O people, to these give glory,
That your name among nations may be great.

IX

How long—for haply not now much longer—
Shall fear put faith in a faithless creed,
And shapes and shadows of truths be stronger
In strong men's eyes than the truth indeed?
If freedom be not a word that dies when spoken,
If justice be not a dream whence men must wake,
How shall not the bonds of the thraldom of old be broken,
And right put might in the hands of them that break?
For clear as a tocsin from the steeple
Is the cry gone forth along the land,
Take heed, ye unwise among the people:
O ye fools, when will ye understand?

A BALLAD AT PARTING

Sea to sea that clasps and fosters England, uttering ever-more
Song eterne and praise immortal of the indomitable shore,
Lifts aloud her constant heart up, south to north and east to west,
Here in speech that shames all music, there in thunder-throated roar,
Chiming concord out of discord, waking rapture out of rest.
All her ways are lovely, all her works and symbols are divine,
Yet shall man love best what first bade leap his heart and bend his knee;
Yet where first his whole soul worshipped shall his soul set up her shrine:
Nor may love not know the lovelier, fair as both beheld may be,
Here the limitless north-eastern, there the strait south-western sea.

Though their chant bear all one burden, as ere man was born it bore;
Though the burden be diviner than the songs all souls adore;
Yet may love not choose but choose between them which to love the best.
Me the sea my nursing-mother, me the Channel green and hoar,
Holds at heart more fast than all things, bares for me the goodlier breast,
Lifts for me the lordlier love-song, bids for me more sunlight shine,
Sounds for me the stormier trumpet of the sweeter strain to me.
So the broad pale Thames is loved not like the tawny springs of Tyne:

Choice is clear between them for the soul whose vision holds in fee
Here the limitless north-eastern, there the strait south-western sea.

Choice is clear, but dear is either; nor has either not in store
Many a likeness, many a written sign of spirit-searching lore,
Whence the soul takes fire of sweet remembrance, magnified and blest.
Thought of songs whose flame-winged feet have trod the unfooted water-floor
When the lord of all the living lords of souls bade speed their quest,
Soft live sound like children's babble down the rippling sand's incline,
Or the lovely song that loves them, hailed with thankful prayer and plea;
These are parcels of the harvest here whose gathered sheaves are mine,
Garnered now, but sown and reaped where winds make wild with wrath or glee
Here the limitless north-eastern, there the strait south-western sea.

Song, thy name is freedom, seeing thy strength was born of breeze and brine.
Fare now forth and fear no fortune; such a seal is set on thee.
Joy begat and memory bare thee, seeing in spirit a two-fold sign,
Even the sign of those thy fosters, each as thou from all time free,
Here the limitless north-eastern, there the strait south-western sea.

Algernon Charles Swinburne – A Short Biography

Algernon Charles Swinburne was born at 7 Chester Street, Grosvenor Place, in London, on April 5th, 1837. He was the eldest of six children born to Captain Charles Henry Swinburne and Lady Jane Henrietta, daughter of the 3rd Earl of Ashburnham, a wealthy Northumbrian family.

Swinburne spent his early years at East Dene in Bonchurch, on the Isle of Wight. As a child, Swinburne was nervous and frail, but also imbued with a nervous energy and fearlessness almost to the point of recklessness.

He was schooled at Eton College from 1849 to 1853. It was here that he first began to write poetry. He excelled at languages and whilst still at Eton won first prizes in both French and Italian.

From Eton he moved to Oxford where he attended at Balliol College from 1856. Here he met friends to whom he became closely attached, among them Dante Gabriel Rossetti, William Morris and Edward Burne-Jones, who in 1857, were painting their Arthurian murals on the walls of the Oxford Union. At Oxford Swinburne was mentored by Benjamin Jowett, the master of Balliol College, who recognised his poetic talent and, intervening on his behalf, tried to keep him from being expelled when he celebrated the Italian patriot Orsini, and his failed attempt on the life of Napoleon III in 1858. Swinburne had to leave the Universcity for a few months due to this but returned in May, 1860 but never received a degree.

Summers were usually spent at Capheaton Hall in Northumberland, the house of his grandfather, Sir John Swinburne, 6th Baronet, who had a famous library and was himself President of the Literary and Philosophical Society in Newcastle upon Tyne.

Swinburne proudly considered himself a native of Northumberland and this is reflected in poems such as the intensely patriotic 'Northumberland' and 'Grace Darling'. He enjoyed riding across the moors and was, it was said, a daring horseman, as he moved 'through honeyed leagues of the northland border', as he remembered the Scottish border in his Recollections.

In the period from 1857 to 1860, Swinburne was one of a number of Pre-Raphaelite's who visited and became part of Lady Pauline Trevelyan's intellectual circle at Wallington Hall, a few miles west of Morpeth in Northumberland.

After leaving college, he moved to London and began his career in earnest as well as becoming a constant visitor to the Rossetti's house. To Rossetti Swinburne was his 'little Northumbrian friend', an affectionate reference to Swinburne's small stature—a mere five foot four. Whatever Swinburne lacked in height he made up for in poetic talent. However, with the burden of such great talent came the unveiling of a dark side that was to cause him pain and would, at times, threaten his very existence with all manner of self-inflicted pains through drink, drugs and sado-machoism.

In 1860 Swinburne published two verse dramas; The Queen Mother and Rosamond but it would not be until 1865 that Swinburne would achieve literary success with Atalanta in Calydon.

In 1861, Swinburne visited Menton on the French Riviera to recover from the effects of yet another period of excess use of alcohol, staying at the Villa Laurenti. From Menton, Swinburne then travelled on to Italy, where he journeyed widely.

After Elizabeth Rossetti's death from suicide in 1862, he and Rossetti moved to Tudor House at 16 Cheyne Walk in Chelsea. The stories that survive from his year with Rossetti are typical Swinburne. In one, Rossetti once had to tell him to keep down the noise — he and a boyfriend had been sliding naked down the bannisters and disturbing Rossetti's painting. He took a sardonic delight in what the critic and biographer, Cecil Lang, calls "Algernonic exaggeration": When people began to talk scathingly about his homosexuality and other sexual proclivities, he circulated a story that he had engaged in pederasty and bestiality with a monkey — and then eaten it. How many of the stories were true and how many invented is unclear. Oscar Wilde called him "a braggart in matters of vice, who had done everything he could to convince his fellow citizens of his homosexuality and bestiality without being in the slightest degree a homosexual or a bestialiser."

In December 1862, Swinburne accompanied Scott and his guests on a trip to Tynemouth. Scott writes in his memoirs that, as they walked by the sea, Swinburne declaimed the as yet unpublished 'Hymn to Proserpine' and 'Laus Veneris' in his lilting intonation, while the waves 'were running the whole length of the long level sands towards Cullercoats and sounding like far-off acclamations'.

Swinburne possessed a curious combination of frail health and strength. He was small and slightly built, but an excellent swimmer and the first to climb Culver Cliff on the Isle of Wight. He had an extremely excitable disposition: people who met him described him as a "demoniac boy" who would go skipping about the room declaiming poetry at the top of his voice. In this as in many things, moderation was not the standard for him. Excess was. Once or twice he had fits, thought to be epileptic, in public; but he made this condition much worse by drinking past excess to unconsciousness. More than once he was delivered to the door in the small of the night, dead drunk. Throughout the 1860s and '70s he rode an alcoholic cycle of dissolution, collapse, drying out at home in the country, then returning to London where he would begin the cycle all over again.

His mania for masochism, particularly flagellation, most probably started in early childhood at Eton and was encouraged by his later friendships with Richard Monckton Milnes (one of Tennyson's fellow Apostles), who introduced him to the works of the Marquis de Sade, and Richard Burton, the Victorian explorer and adventurer. Swinburne was an alcoholic and algolagniac (a desire for sexual gratification through inflicting pain on oneself or others; sadomasochism). He found life difficult, unfulfilling but still his poetic talents pushed to the fore.

Although Swinburne continued to publish some works in periodicals in 1865 he was granted recognition by both public and critics with Atalanta in Calydon written in the style of a classical Greek tragedy.

There followed "Laus Veneris" and Poems and Ballads (1866), with their sexually charged passages, absolutely decadent for polite Victorian society, which were attacked all the more violently as a result. The poems written in homage of Sappho of Lesbos such as "Anactoria" and "Sapphics" were especially savaged. The volume also contained poems such as "The Leper," "Laus Veneris," and "St Dorothy" which evoke both Swinburne's and a general Victorian fascination with the Middle Ages, and are explicitly mediaeval in style, tone and construction. With its publication came instant notoriety. He was now identified with indecent and decadent themes and the precept of art for art's sake.

Swinburne's meeting in 1867 with his long-time hero Mazzini, the Italian patriot living in England in exile, was the beginning of a poetical journey that now became more serious and more engaged with serious thought, initially leading to the political poems in the volume Songs Before Sunrise.

Also in 1867 he was introduced to Adah Isaacs Menken, the American actress, poet and circus rider, whose main fame seemed to be riding naked on a horse (in fact she wore tight nude coloured clothing) for her performance in the melodrama Mazeppa (itself based on a poem by Lord Byron). Although they had a short affair Adah's quote implies that Swinburne was not ready for a relationship that did not involve some self-sabotage; "I can't make him understand that biting's no use."

In 1879, with Swinburne nearly dead from alcoholism and dissolution, his legal advisor Theodore Watts-Dunton took him in, and was gradually successful in getting him to adapt to a healthier lifestyle. Swinburne lived the rest of his life at Watts-Dunton's house. He saw less and less of his old bohemian friends, who thought him a prisoner at The Pines, but his growing deafness also accounts for some of his decreased sociability. By now Swinburne was 42, and was moving from a young man of rebelliousness to a figure of social respectability. It was said of Watts-Dunton that he saved the man and killed the poet.

It is clear that Swinburne had an addictive personality, and clearly incapable of moderation in his pursuit of any chosen vices. This, of course, would both nourish and perhaps sabotage his poetic career. His poetry follows the somewhat clichéd pattern of early flourish and later decline; indeed some of the fresher pieces in the second and third series of Poems and Ballads (published in 1878 and 1889) were actually written during his days at Oxford. Nevertheless, his last collection, A Channel Passage, has some beautiful poems, including "The Lake of Gaube."

He is best remembered as the supreme technician in metre, with a versatility which exceeds even Tennyson's, but which lacks a corresponding emotional range. His obsessions are not widely enough shared; and if he cannot shock us by the strangeness of his desires nor the shrillness of his anti-theistical exclamations, often what remains is not enough to fully engage with the audience.

Swinburne is considered a poet of the decadent school, although he perhaps professed to more vice than he actually indulged in to advertise his deviance. Common gossip of the time reported that he also had a deep crush on the explorer Sir Richard Francis Burton, despite the fact that Swinburne himself abhorred travel. Fact and fiction are easily absorbed by the other so are difficult to untangle even now.

Many critics consider his mastery of vocabulary, rhyme and metre impressive, although he has also been criticised for his florid style and word choices that only fit the rhyme scheme rather than contributing to the meaning of the piece. A. E. Housman, although a critic, had great praise for his rhyming ability: to Swinburne the sonnet was child's play: the task of providing four rhymes was not hard enough, and he wrote long poems in which each stanza required eight or ten rhymes, and wrote them so that he never seemed to be saying anything for the rhyme's sake.

Throughout his career Swinburne published literary criticism of great worth. His deep knowledge of world literatures contributed to a critical style rich in quotation, allusion, and comparison. He is particularly noted for discerning studies of Elizabethan dramatists and of many English and French poets and novelists. As well he was a noted essayist and wrote two novels.

Swinburne was nominated for the Nobel Prize in Literature every year from 1903 to 1907 and then again in 1909.

H.P. Lovecraft, the master of the dark side and a decent poet himself, considered Swinburne "the only real poet in either England or America after the death of Mr. Edgar Allan Poe."

Swinburne was also responsible for devising a poetic form called the roundel, a variation of the French Rondeau form. In 1883 he published A Century of Roundels with several of the roundels dedicated to Dante's sister, the poet Christina Georgina Rossetti. Swinburne wrote to Edward Burne-Jones in 1883: "I have got a tiny new book of songs or songlets, in one form and all manner of metres ... just coming out, of which Miss Rossetti has accepted the dedication. I hope you and Georgie [his wife Georgiana] will find something to like among a hundred poems of nine lines each, twenty-four of which are about babies or small children".

Opinions of the Roundel poems move between those who find them captivating and brilliant, to others who find them merely clever and contrived. One of them, A Baby's Death, was set to music by the English composer Sir Edward Elgar as the song "Roundel: The little eyes that never knew Light".

After the first Poems and Ballads, Swinburne's later poetry was devoted more to philosophy and politics, including the unification of Italy, particularly in the volume Songs before Sunrise. He did not stop writing love poetry entirely, indeed it was only in 1882 that his great epic-length poem, Tristram of Lyonesse, was published, its contents lyrical rather than shocking. His versification, and especially his rhyming technique, remain of high quality to the end.

Algernon Charles Swinburne died of influenza, at the Pines in London on April 10th, 1909 at the age of 72. He was buried at St. Boniface Church, Bonchurch on the Isle of Wight.

The Queen Mother (1860)
Rosamond (1860)
Chastelard (1865)
Bothwell (1874)
Mary Stuart (1881)
Marino Faliero (1885)
Locrine (1887)
The Sisters (1892)
Rosamund, Queen of the Lombards (1899)

Poetry
Atalanta in Calydon (1865)*
Poems and Ballads (1866)
Songs Before Sunrise (1871)
Songs of Two Nations (1875)
Erechtheus (1876)*
Poems and Ballads, Second Series (1878)
Songs of the Springtides (1880)
Studies in Song (1880)
The Heptalogia, or the Seven against Sense. A Cap with Seven Bells (1880)
Tristram of Lyonesse (1882)
A Dark Month & Other Poems
A Century of Roundels (1883)
A Midsummer Holiday and Other Poems (1884)
Poems and Ballads, Third Series (1889)
Astrophel and Other Poems (1894)
The Tale of Balen (1896)
A Channel Passage and Other Poems (1904)

*Although formally tragedies, Atlanta in Calydon and Erechtheus are traditionally included with his poetry.

Criticism
William Blake: A Critical Essay (1868, new edition 1906)
Under the Microscope (1872)
George Chapman: A Critical Essay (1875)
Essays and Studies (1875)
A Note on Charlotte Brontë (1877)
A Study of Shakespeare (1880)
A Study of Victor Hugo (1886)
A Study of Ben Johnson (1889)
Studies in Prose and Poetry (1894)
The Age of Shakespeare (1908)
Shakespeare (1909)

Major Collections
The Poems of Algernon Charles Swinburne, 6 vols. 1904.

The Tragedies of Algernon Charles Swinburne, 5 vols. 1905.
The Complete Works of Algernon Charles Swinburne, 20 vols. Bonchurch Edition. 1925-7.
The Swinburne Letters, 6 vols. 1959-62.